A1 DINER

In memory of Karen Mølvig,
who introduced me to the remarkable A1 Diner

And to my friends in Maine; I love you all very much

A 1 DINER

Real Food, Recipes, & Recollections

Sarah Rolph

Photography by Jeff Giberson

Tilbury House, Publishers • Gardiner, Maine

TILBURY HOUSE 🏠 PUBLISHERS
2 Mechanic Street
Gardiner, Maine 04345
800–582–1899 • www.tilburyhouse.com

First edition: July 2006 • 10 9 8 7 6 5 4 3 2 1

Recipe for Hungarian Mushroom Soup reprinted with permission from *The New Moosewood Cookbook* by Mollie Katzen. Copyright 1977, 1992, 2000 by Tante Malka, Inc., Ten Speed Press, Berkeley, CA. www.tenspeed.com.

Library of Congress Cataloging-in-Publication Data
Rolph, Sarah, 1955-
  A1 diner : real food, recipes, and recollections / by Sarah Rolph ;
photography by Jeff Giberson. -- 1st ed.
      p. cm.
  Includes index.
  ISBN-13: 978-0-88448-277-2 (pbk. : alk. paper)
  ISBN-10: 0-88448-277-4 (pbk. : alk. paper)
  1. Cookery, American--New England style. 2. A1 Diner. I. Title.
  TX715.2.N48R66 2006
  641.5'974--dc22
                                        2006014556

Cover painting by Ruthanne Harrison, Richmond, Maine
Designed on Crummett Mountain by Edith Allard, Somerville, Maine
Project Editor: Julie Eubanks
Copyediting by Gay Grant, The Write Way, Gardiner, Maine
Covers printed by the John P. Pow Company, South Boston
Text printed and bound by Maple Vail, Kirkwood, New York

CONTENTS

RECIPES

Side Dishes

Desserts

ONE

The Early Years

1. All the New Songs, Like Glenn Miller

THE DINER IS SMALL. The counter seats sixteen, and six booths line the windows. Entering the small space is a visual adjustment, like walking into a playhouse. Everything is close at hand.

The countertops are large slabs of pink marble, cool to the touch. Behind the counter, where the grill once stood, the walls are shining stainless steel, pleated in a sunburst design. Cut in that back wall is a small window to the kitchen, through which the orders are sent and the food is received. The floor is a mosaic of small black-and-white tiles. Where the counter opens to let the wait staff scurry through, rounded glass blocks create a graceful curve.

The booths are made of mahogany and upholstered in blue leatherette. The tables show decades of wear. Thousands of wrists and elbows have rested here, next to thousands of plates and cups.

Windows extend around three sides of the diner, and below them, the walls are tiled in blue. The trim around the windows and above them is mahogany. The ceiling is made of wood and blue Formica.

June 5, 2006, marked sixty years since Worcester Diner #790 arrived at 3 Bridge Street in Gardiner, Maine. Born as Heald's, the diner retains that name on its side, indelibly baked into the diner's porcelain exterior.

In 1946 Worcester Diners were at their height. The company had been manufacturing the self-contained diners since 1906, building on a previous innovation. Night-shift workers in the bustling East Coast factories of the late 1800s had no place to eat until an enterprising young man named Walter Scott created the lunch wagon, a horse-drawn enclosed carriage from which sandwiches and coffee were available to take away. "Night lunch" was a big hit in factory towns, and soon the horse-drawn lunch wagons proliferated. By the early 1900s they included a compact cooking area, and patrons could sit inside on stools along a wooden counter. By the 1930s the lunch wagon had evolved into the dining car, so named as an allusion to railroad cars, which they were created to resemble, since trains at the time were the most glamorous of modern conveyances.

Worcester Diners were hand-built at the factory, then transported to their sites with a large truck. Irene Wise remembers when the diner arrived in Gardiner: "One of the things all us teenagers wondered was how it was going to stay up in the position on the bridge," she relates. "We all hesitated to go in for fear it would fall into the stream. We didn't trust the underpinning to hold."

Each Worcester Diner was given a number at the factory, providing a historical record of the order in which they were built.

The diner's location is certainly unusual. Perched next to the bridge over Cobbossee Stream, it sits about 20 feet above the ground on a nest of steel girders built specifically to support it. There is just enough room for the diner to fit between the bridge and the building behind it. This curious arrangement is the result of change over time.

The building behind the diner, now largely hidden, once extended up to the bridge, and was the site of a mechanic's garage. In 1937 Eddie Heald took over the building and created a small wooden diner. What had been the office and parts room became the dining room, and the section of the building that had been used for repairs became the kitchen.

That twelve-seat wooden diner, officially called the Bridge Street Lunch, "wasn't much bigger than a smelt shack," says Walter Gosline, who had coffee and donuts there every morning, along with a few other regulars including his best friend Dan Chapman, Sr.

When Heald purchased his Worcester Diner, he had the front of the building cut off to make room for it, and the steel girders were put in place by Ralph Dick of Gardiner's T. W. Dick steel company. A close look at the building today reveals where the front was sliced off, creating just enough room for the diner.

When Heald's Diner arrived in Gardiner, it drew comment. "We thought it was elegant," says Gosline. "We hadn't seen anything like it. It was all done so nicely—the counter, the stools, the booths—it was pretty fancy for those days."

The diner sits hard up against the modified building, which houses today's kitchen. The entrance to the kitchen is on the side of the building, down a narrow wooden walkway—the same walkway and the same kitchen door that Walter Gosline entered when he delivered milk to the diner in the 1940s, 1950s, and 1960s.

Because of its strange heritage as a former garage, the diner's kitchen is ample. It's much bigger than the diner itself, in fact. A meandering space, it features several rooms, each leading to the next.

The front part of the kitchen, just visible from the diner itself through the little pass-through window, is where the short-order cooking is done—eggs and home fries at breakfast, hamburgers and French fries at lunch. This is the "hot line." Walking past the hot line, one comes to a large side area where the dishwashers toil. There is a large, old dishwashing machine here, but the pots and pans are done by hand at huge sinks amid great clouds of steam. Behind that area is a workstation off to itself, where Matt Rowe makes the sushi. And next to that, around the corner from the grill, is where the "prep cooks" work—those who do the food preparation (as opposed to the "line cooks" who do the short-order cooking). In the prep area, there are large wooden tables with several workstations and another large stove. In and among these work areas are storage shelves, bins of utensils, pots and pans, closets with big bags of potatoes and onions, and an old-fashioned potato cutter that has been used for decades to make the hand-cut fries.

Today it's a bustling area, with a lot of food being prepared—not only the extensive menu of A1 Diner, but also the takeout food for A1 To Go next door. The large kitchen came in handy for making roasts and doing food preparation in the early days, as well.

But when the diner first came to town in 1946, all of the line cooking was done in the diner itself, at the grill and steam table located behind the counter. Those are gone now, but the original biscuit warmer is still there, and still in use.

Each diner was built according to specification from a long list of available elements. An original "Cost Sheet for Construction of Diners," now at the Worcester Historical Museum, details the elements involved—the steel for the platform and body; the ceiling panels, hardware, and windows; the counters, stools, booths, and hat trees; the grill, fryolator, pie-rack shelves, and menu signs. Costs and notes are entered by hand in pencil. The Worcester company contracted some of the work to local tradesmen and craftsmen. "By Floyd Severy" it says on the cost sheet next to "Electric Wiring." "By Bianchi" it says, next to "Tile and Marble Work."

Eddie Heald's daughter, Marguerite (now Marguerite Gagne), remembers going to Worcester with her dad to order the diner, specifying the components from the Worcester catalog. "That diner was the best one you could buy," she says. "That was the top of the line."

Marguerite started working for her dad in 1941 when she was just nine years old. Like most other diner employees both then and now, she started as a dishwasher. She began waiting tables when she turned eleven. Today she remembers the diner fondly, but at the time, she often wished she were elsewhere.

"I spent many hours working there. I didn't like it. But I did it. I wanted to be out with my friends, but it was a family business," says Marguerite. "I used to work my lunch hour and then go back up to school. After school I would come down to work the supper hour. Kids today don't know what it's like to work. And no rides! I walked!"

There was one part of working at the diner Marguerite enjoyed. "We used to put on a banquet every year for the football team," she remembers. "I used to like that. Boys! I'd say, well, I'll wait on them!"

Marguerite also enjoyed being the one to pick out the records for the jukeboxes that the diner used to have on every table. She would select her favorites, she says, "All the new songs, like Glenn Miller."

Worcester Diners were built at the factory to the customer's specifications. This hand-drawn floor plan from 1946 shows the exact placement of everything in the original Heald's Diner. The handwritten notes provide details that in many cases had been forgotten—we see, for example, that the counter is made of Tennessee marble. The notes also tell us about the language used at the time to describe the architectural details. "Stainless steel with Rays," for example, is how the pleated sunburst design was specified. And what we now call the menu board was known as the "Bill of Fare." IMAGE COURTESY OF THE DINER ARCHIVES OF RICHARD J. S. GUTMAN.

Left: Custom steel underpinnings hold the diner at street level. Many an early customer wondered if these steel underpinnings would hold.

Below: When Heald's Diner first came to Gardiner, there was no railing on the bridge, affording a clear view of the Heald's name on the diner's porcelain exterior. This photo was taken on June 5, 1946 when the diner was being installed.
Photos courtesy of the Diner Archives of Richard J. S. Gutman

All the New Songs, Like Glen Miller

Speaking of Fried Clams

Ours are the very best.

STOP AND TRY THEM

We're also serving Fried Scallops and regular dinners.

Quick Service if you're in a hurry — or take your time in our restful atmosphere.

Bridge St. Lunch

E. H. HEALD, Prop.
Gardiner

Before the diner arrived at 3 Bridge Street in 1946, Eddie Heald was the proprietor of the twelve-seat Bridge Street Lunch in the same location. COURTESY OF MARGUERITE GAGNE

HOME MADE PASTRY

... Try Our Delicious Hamburgs ...

BRIDGE STREET LUNCH

EDDIE H. HEALD, Prop.

BRIDGE STREET, GARDINER, MAINE

SPECIAL DINNERS 35¢

A Special New Menu Each Day

An original postcard from the Heald's Diner era. COURTESY OF MARGUERITE GAGNE

Like the Bridge Street Lunch before it, Heald's Diner fed the
workers of Gardiner, employees of the paper and cotton mills and the
shoe factories that made Gardiner a busy industrial center in the early
to mid twentieth century. The emphasis was on ample portions served
quickly.

"We got them in and out," says Marguerite. "You took the orders
and they came right out. We would cook three or four meals a day.
Roast pork, ham, things like that. My dad was a wonderful cook. He
had roasts every day. And everything was from scratch. He made the
pies, turnovers, donuts—and I mean, beautiful. Nothing in a package
or anything. People used to line up way down around the corner at
Manson & Church's to get in that diner."

Today Marguerite lives in Augusta, Maine, not far from Gardiner.
When we wanted a photo for this book of Marguerite at the diner, A1
Diner co-owner Mike Giberson opened up on a holiday—just for
her—and made a special brunch: individual cheese soufflés. During the
visit, she marveled at how little the diner has changed.

She recognized the coffee mugs—Mike served her in an original
mug, which varies slightly from the newer ones. Most of us wouldn't

All the New Songs, Like Glen Miller

Right: Eddie Heald, the first owner of the diner, with his daughter Marguerite. This photo was taken at a carnival in 1946. COURTESY OF MARGUERITE GAGNE

Below: Marguerite with Mike Giberson, a current co-owner of the diner. This photo was taken in 2005.
PHOTO BY HANNAH HARDING

be able to tell the difference, but Mike and Marguerite can. (The old mugs are a little larger, and a little heavier, and their shape is slightly different.) The two of them couldn't stop talking about all the details that have stayed the same all these years. The menu boards are the same. The waitresses who have to change those little white letters every day still complain about it, as Marguerite did. And the letters themselves are still kept in the same old green wooden box.

"It feels so familiar," said Marguerite. "Just like home."

Individual Cheese Soufflés

4 SERVINGS

Mike created these individual cheese soufflés to honor Marguerite Gagne with a special brunch. The serving looks large, but the soufflé is so light, one manages easily to eat every bite.

3 tablespoons butter
3 tablespoons flour
1 cup hot milk
5 egg yolks
1 tablespoon dry mustard
1 teaspoon chopped parsley
1 teaspoon chopped chives
2 cups Swiss or Gruyere cheese, grated
salt and freshly ground black pepper, to taste
5 egg whites, at room temperature
pinch salt

Heat the oven to 375° F. Butter 4 large ramekins (individual soufflé dishes, 4-inch diameter).

Melt the butter in a heavy medium-sized saucepan over medium heat. When it starts to foam, add the flour, reduce heat to low, and cook, stirring constantly, for about 2 minutes.

Gradually whisk in the milk. Cook, stirring constantly, until smooth and thick, about 3 minutes.

Remove from the heat and add the egg yolks, one at a time, whisking well after each addition.

Stir in the mustard, parsley, chives, and cheese. Add the salt and pepper.

Beat the egg whites with a pinch of salt until stiff but not dry.

Stir one third of the beaten egg whites into the yolk-cheese mixture. Then fold the remaining beaten whites into the mixture (that is, incorporate them carefully by lifting and turning the batter, without beating; a flexible spatula works well for this task).

Pour the batter into the buttered ramekins, filling each about two-thirds full. Bake until well puffed and golden, about 45 minutes. Serve immediately.

2. Yankee Soul Food

BOB NEWELL LIKES TO JOKE that he has been "sold" three times. Maurice Wakefield was the first to "buy" Bob, when he purchased the diner from Eddie Heald in 1952, just six years after the new, modern diner came to town.

Maurice and Bob worked side by side for twenty-five years, with Bob on the grill. They still keep in touch. "We're still together, emotionally," says Maurice. Now in his nineties and living in Zephyrhills, Florida, Maurice remembers the diner fondly.

"On the left behind the counter is where the grill was, and the fryolator," says Maurice. "On the right was the steam table. That's where we served, right there. Everything hot was kept on the steam table—the meat loaf and the macaroni and cheese and all. Out back there was practically nothing but a dishwasher and two nice work tables."

Later, the grill was moved back into the kitchen to discourage cooks from chatting too much. "When business picked up it was hard to get a short-order cook I could turn my back on," says Maurice. "The cooks were always talking to their friends and their family. I'm not talking about Bob, now. Bob was working in the morning. The other guys who worked from noon on, they were the problem."

"So I moved the grill and the steam table out back. They had always had a pass-through for the dirty dishes, down low, so I had a passage cut on top for sending the food out. I cut that through. We would tap the bell when the food was ready, and the girl would come get it at the window. That worked pretty good. And it kept the short-order cooks from visiting with their friends all the time."

That little window between the counter and the kitchen has been a defining feature of the diner ever since.

Soon after Maurice purchased the diner, he hired Cindy DeLong to work for him. She was just fifteen years old. Like most diner employees, Cindy started as a dishwasher, but Maurice encouraged her to come out front and work as a waitress. "I had a hard time with that," says Cindy, who still lives in Gardiner (she retired from the diner in 2004). "I was shy, bashful; I don't have the gift of gab. I still have a hard time talking to people. But eventually I got over it, and I starting working in front."

When Cindy started working at the diner, Gardiner was still a factory town, and speed was of the essence. "They could get a meal out of the kitchen in a minute," Cindy remembers. "They had a steam table, with whatever the special was that day, maybe it was meatloaf, and

Built in 1946, the diner's architectural details are largely Art Moderne.

they had a hot vegetable and a potato, and it was all ready, so it would take them less than a minute to get that meal out."

Cindy had a lot of patience for the tricks people liked to play on her.

"Danny Chapman, across the street, he's one who came over here and pulled a lot of tricks," says Cindy. "I drink black coffee, and I used to have my own cup right on the counter there. I never finished it, I'd just keep adding to it. So at the end of the day when I would drink it up, there would be an old nut or bolt in the bottom that Danny had dumped in there during the day. I don't know how many cups of coffee I had on top of some old nail or whatever, and here I was drinking those germs all day long."

The food was hearty and the portions were large. On Friday the special was fish chowder. "It wasn't all juice, either," says Maurice. "It was a lot of fish and potatoes. It was a meal in itself, with some crackers and dessert."

Beef stew was always on the menu: "I made big five-gallon batches of it. That, too, was a meal in itself. I didn't just drag a little meat through it—that was a heavy stew," says Maurice.

And there was a wide variety of fish. "Another thing they liked a lot was baked, stuffed whitefish. We actually used cusk. It looked like halibut but it wasn't—it was cusk. That name didn't sound so good so I called it whitefish."

"But no matter what people like, they like a change," Maurice observes. "So I also served a halibut in cream sauce; it must have been an egg sauce. And in season, I served baked mackerel. We served oysters, fried or in oyster stew. That oyster stew we served fresh. And we served fried clams. Not strip clams. I never sold strip clams in my life. We served clams with a belly on them."

"In the wintertime we had smelts. We would get a five-gallon pail of them; I'll tell you, I was busy cleaning those little rascals."

The diner still serves smelts occasionally, in season—which starts when the river freezes and ends when the river thaws. The Kennebec River near Gardiner is one of the last best places to find smelt—they're still being caught there, on a good day, by the bucketful. In New England, ice fishing is considered a venerable pastime; reportedly, beer is involved. Ice-fishing cabins ("smelt shacks") are set up around the hole in the ice through which the fishing lines are dropped. The term for a batch of these small fish is a "mess of smelt."

"My most popular dish was macaroni and cheese," says Maurice. "You notice I didn't say baked macaroni. The way I did it, I cooked the macaroni, drained it, and put it in a dish with cheese, then blended it with a spoon so the cheese got all over, and then I diluted it with milk. You use just enough milk for it to be soft. Not too runny, but not all hard like baked macaroni can be. Just right."

Today the diner still serves macaroni and cheese, both the traditional style—which is still not baked—and Mike's splendid variations.

Among the many parallels between Maurice Wakefield and the diner's current owners, Michael Giberson and Neil Anderson, is a shared sensibility about the importance of quality ingredients. Mike and Neil have taken the menu much further in this direction, with fine-food specialties that feature fresh, local food whenever possible, but Maurice is just as proud of the food he served. "I used the very best stuff I could buy," he says. "The best vegetables, the best Dutch cocoa—little things like that make a difference."

When he first started running the diner, says Maurice, "all they wanted for vegetables was canned peas and beans. I wanted to fix turnips and squash and fresh vegetables. Well, I did train them eventually to eat the good, old Maine food."

Maurice has a term for his home-style cooking. "At the time I considered myself a woods cook," he says. "In those days people would work in the woods all summer and they needed good food and plenty of it. But as time went on we learned about Southern cooking and so on and we created a style of our own—Yankee Soul Food, that's what we were doing, without knowing it."

Top, left: The stainless steel "rays" on the back wall of the diner. Bottom, left: These mahogany storage bins are built into the diner's ceiling. Right: The original biscuit warmer, still in use.

Fried Smelts

4 SERVINGS (allow about six 6-inch smelts per person)
Fried smelts are a New England tradition. The Kennebec River, which runs past Gardiner, is one of the best places to catch these fish. The smelt season begins when the river freezes and ends when the river thaws; the fish are caught through the ice. Serious smelt fans, it is said, take their frying pans and cornmeal mix with them onto the ice, then cook their catch on a pot-bellied stove in the smelt shack, or even on a fire built on the ice — the Kennebec freezes that thick in the winter.

24 cleaned smelts, heads removed, each about 6 inches long (if your smelts are
  smaller, you may wish to increase the number of smelts per person)
1/2 cup flour
1 cup fine cornmeal
1 teaspoon salt
freshly ground black pepper to taste (about 1/2 teaspoon to start)
vegetable oil

Heat the vegetable oil to 350° F in a deep fryer, or in a frying pan (if using a pan, use about one inch of oil).

Mix together the flour, cornmeal, salt, and pepper. Roll the smelts in the flour mixture.

When the oil is hot, fry the smelts just until done, about 2 or 3 minutes. (For smaller smelts, cook them not quite as long.)

The fish is done when the meat is opaque.

Not Baked Macaroni and Cheese

6 SERVINGS

The macaroni and cheese at the diner has not changed much over the years. Maurice Wakefield was a firm believer in serving this dish without baking it, in order to preserve its creamy texture and keep it from drying out. Mike and Neil have the same philosophy.

1 pound elbow macaroni
6 tablespoons butter
3 tablespoons flour
3/4 teaspoon salt
3/4 teaspoon white pepper
2 1/2 cups milk, heated until warm but not boiling
1/2 pound grated white American or cheddar cheese

Bring a large pot of salted water to a boil. Cook the macaroni until just done, about 10 minutes. Drain and rinse under cold water.

While the macaroni is cooking, melt the butter in a small saucepan. Add the flour and cook, stirring over low heat about 5 minutes, without browning.

Slowly add milk, stirring. Stir until smooth and thick, about 5 minutes. Add the grated cheese.

Return the drained pasta to the pot. Stir in the cheese mixture to mix. (The heat of the pasta will finish melting the cheese.) Serve hot.

In the diner, Mike uses whatever cheese is available in the kitchen and needs to be used up. Home cooks may wish to do the same, using whatever is at hand. Or use your favorite cheese, or try a mixture of cheeses.

On the recipe used in the A1 kitchen, there is a notation: Do not use black pepper in this dish. Many people prefer to use only white pepper in light-colored dishes; others don't mind the specks. In your kitchen, it is your choice.

Macaroni with Italian Cheeses, Peas, and Prosciutto

6 SERVINGS

This easy macaroni and cheese variation is quick to prepare, making it an ideal weekday supper.

1 pound elbow macaroni (or any shape of pasta)
1 small onion, diced
2 tablespoons olive oil
2 medium garlic cloves, finely chopped
1/2 pound prosciutto, finely chopped (you may substitute any ham for the
  prosciutto, although the flavor will not be quite the same)
1 pound grated mixed Italian cheeses, such as Italian Fontina and Parmigiano-
  Reggiano
1 10-ounce package frozen peas, thawed
freshly ground black pepper (optional)

Bring a large pot of salted water to boil. Cook the pasta until just done, about 10 minutes.

While the pasta is cooking, cook the onion in the olive oil over medium heat for about five minutes, until soft. Add the garlic and stir, cooking another minute or two, just until fragrant. Add the prosciutto to the pan, stir, and turn off the heat.

When the pasta is ready, drain it and return it to the pot. Add the grated cheese and stir. (The heat of the pasta will melt the cheese.) Add the peas and the onion-garlic-prosciutto mixture. Stir. Serve immediately, with freshly ground black pepper if desired.

⚜ Use a mix of soft cheese, such as Fontina, and hard tangy cheeses, such as Parmesan or Asiago. The best kind of Parmesan is Parmigiano-Reggiano, which is named for the region in Italy in which it is made.

Mrs. Wakefield's Gingerless Gingerbread

10–12 SERVINGS

Maurice Wakefield's wife, Edith, was widely known as a good cook. This recipe for gingerbread was originally hers. Maurice increased the proportions for use in the diner, and we have reduced them back to the original size for the home cook.

$^1/2$ cup sugar
$^1/2$ teaspoon salt
2 teaspoons baking soda
$^1/2$ teaspoon nutmeg
1 teaspoon cinnamon
$^1/4$ teaspoon cloves
2 eggs
1 cup molasses
$^1/2$ cup vegetable oil or melted shortening
$2^1/2$ cups flour
$^1/2$ cup hot water

Heat the oven to 400° F.

Grease a 9 x 13-inch pan.

In a small bowl, mix together the sugar, salt, baking soda, nutmeg, cinnamon, and cloves.

In a large bowl, beat the eggs with the molasses. Add the vegetable oil or melted shortening and the flour and stir to combine. Add the sugar and spice mixture, and stir to combine. Add the hot water and stir.

Pour the batter into the pan and bake for 35–40 minutes.

✺ Maurice says, "Use a nice mild molasses for this, not that black-strap molasses that'll curl your hair." He used pastry flour for this cake, but all-purpose flour will work just fine.

Gingerbread with Lemon Sauce

8 LARGE SERVINGS

Lemon and ginger is a classic flavor combination. This dessert is very popular at the diner today. The use of both fresh and ground ginger gives it a pronounced, spicy ginger flavor that contrasts nicely with the lemon.

16 tablespoons butter (2 sticks), softened
1 cup brown sugar
1/2 cup molasses
1/2 cup light corn syrup
2 eggs, beaten
1/2 teaspoon salt
2 1/2 cups flour
2 teaspoons baking soda
1 cup buttermilk, at room temperature
8 ounces fresh ginger, minced
1 tablespoon ground ginger

Heat the oven to 325° F. Butter a 13 x 9 x 2-inch pan.

In a large bowl, combine the butter and the sugar. Add the molasses, corn syrup, eggs, and salt, and beat until smooth.

Mix together the flour and the baking soda. Using a whisk, mix half of the flour mixture into the butter-sugar-egg mixture, then mix in half of the buttermilk. Whisk in the rest of the flour mixture, then the rest of the buttermilk.

Pour the batter into the prepared pan and bake for 40–45 minutes, until the center is puffed.

Cool, cut into squares, and serve with the lemon sauce.

⁂ Fresh ginger is very stringy. To mince it successfully, first cut the peeled ginger into coins, then mince the coins. Cutting it crosswise into coins severs the stringy fibers, which run the length of the ginger root.

Lemon Sauce

This lemon sauce is outrageously good (but rich). You will end up with 12 unused egg whites. Use them to make meringues or an angel food cake.

grated peel of 1 lemon
1 cup lemon juice
1 1/2 cups sugar
1/2 teaspoon salt
6 eggs
12 egg yolks
16 tablespoons butter (2 sticks), cut into pieces

Place grated lemon peel, lemon juice, sugar, salt, eggs, and egg yolks in a stainless steel bowl over boiling water (or use a double boiler, if you have one). Keep the water simmering, but not boiling.

Stir with a whisk, continuously, for about 12 minutes, until thick. (The time will vary depending on how hot the water is and how close to the water your bowl is.)

Remove from the heat and, using a whisk, add the butter, piece by piece. Cool the lemon sauce and serve with the gingerbread.

Maurice Wakefield

Maurice Wakefield owned the diner longer than anyone has so far, from 1952 to 1979. Before purchasing the diner, Maurice was a cook for thirteen years at Hubbard's restaurant in Gardiner. Then he had the lunch concession at the Gardiner shoe factories—he would cook all the food at home and then bring it into the lunchroom. Maurice, who turned ninety in 2005, lives in Zephyrhills, Florida, with his daughter Barbara.

I'M PARTIAL TO THE POOR PEOPLE. I'm a person who grew up poor. At the time I had the diner, Gardiner had two shoe shops and two paper mills, so there were lots of working people. I created an atmosphere of the Golden Rule: Treat everyone the way you want to be treated. The patrons, the employees, the salespeople I dealt with—it was always a family attitude.

In those days, poor people who deserved a check from the state didn't get much. So when it ran out, I would just let them sign the guest check. Then when they had a little money again, they would pay me.

I enjoyed dealing with the working man; that was my goal, to take care of him. I could give them the food they needed at a price they could afford. It was a fast situation, but without throwing it at them. I treated them just like the rich people—they were just as good as the rich people. If the rich people, the lawyers, wanted to come in, we would treat them right, too.

When you walked into the diner, you got cold water. You didn't have to ask for it.

I made an outstanding gravy. I learned how to make real gravy from Joe McClain when I worked at Hubbard's. He was a black man who worked there; he taught me a lot. I'll never forget him. I learned the difference from him between good food and excellent food. He showed me how to make gravy; he called it a "roux."

I also had a friend who was a baker. He taught me to make pie crusts and biscuits. Frank Rice was his name. He had a small bakery in Richmond. On my day off I'd go down to Richmond to learn how to bake.

Those two men made a difference. They knew how to cook. Both these men were very important in my experience.

When the shoe shops left, that rattled us. But it leveled off. I missed the people, but my business held up. I was a tough customer to beat.

I gave the people the best I knew how, and it worked. I have no regrets. I really loved my time there.

꙰ A roux (pronounced "roo") is a mixture of flour and fat (butter, oil, or meat or poultry drippings) that is cooked together before adding liquid. Cooking the flour with the fat eliminates the raw taste of the flour. It also creates a foundation that allows the liquid to be successfully incorporated and thickened, creating a pleasant consistency.

Roux is the starting point for outstanding gravy, as well as for many sauces. White sauce, often called by its French name, béchamel, begins with a roux of butter and flour, in roughly equal portions. The roux is cooked for a few minutes but not browned, then completed with the addition of milk. White sauce is the base for many dishes, such as traditional macaroni and cheese and soufflé. Add cheese to your white sauce, such as Parmesan and/or Swiss, and you have a Mornay sauce (some would say it needs an egg yolk, as well, to be a classic Mornay sauce). A similar sauce using broth and cream is called a velouté sauce. All are built from the same simple principle of the roux.

For a brown sauce or gravy, the roux can be cooked until it is deep golden brown to add a nutty complexity to the flavor of the finished sauce. Roux for Creole dishes such as gumbo is made with oil and cooked for a long time to a deep mahogany brown.

Cindy DeLong

For many customers, Cindy is synonymous with the diner. She worked for three of the owners, starting with Maurice Wakefield in 1962 when she was just fifteen years old. She then worked for Al Giberson and then for the current owners Mike and Neil. Every diner owner has marveled at Cindy's cheerful professionalism and her strong work ethic. "Her hands were never empty," says Mike. To the sorrow of all, Cindy retired from the diner December 31, 2004.

YEARS AGO YOU COULD GET A WHOLE MEAL for under a dollar. When I started here coffee was a dime and donuts were a nickel. I remember when Wakefield raised the price of pie from fifteen cents to twenty-five cents. That must have been in about 1965. I said, "Maurice Wakefield is never going to sell a piece of pie for twenty-five cents!" And what is it today, about three dollars?

I used to just love bouncing out of bed and going to work. My husband used to say, "You're not going to work, you don't feel good." He could tell when I didn't feel good, and he would try to make me stay home. And when we had ice storms he would say, "You're not going out in this," but ice storm or snowstorm, I would say I gotta get there.

A lot of the high school kids would hang out here in the 1950s and 1960s. We had jukeboxes then on every table and on the counter, and the kids would play the music and scream and holler after school.

They would pull all sorts of pranks. They would put my tip in a glass of water upside down. And they'd take the salt shakers and dump out the salt and make the salt shaker stand up in the salt. One girl one time took the squeeze bottle of ketchup and drew a picture on the counter. She was so proud of that. What a mess. But she turned out to be a good kid. They all did, really. I was young, too, so it didn't bother me much.

Some of them were really wild. But they were just young and full of life, and they had been in school all day.

It was a nice time when the kids used to hang out here. And now they're bringing their kids and grandkids in.

Years ago, Friday night here was like Boston or New York. People would go down and park on the street, people would be walking and saying hello to neighbors, and it was packed. They would park, eat here, and then go shopping....

When McDonald's came, in the 1970s, the kids stopped hanging out here. There were some hard times for Gardiner in the 1970s—

when Woolworth's went out, and Grant's went out, and the shoe shops went out, and the movie theater in Randolph went out. People were going to Portland to the big stores.

It's looking a lot better now, there's more on the street. We have Reny's, which is good. Gardiner is coming back.

Albert Giberson, known as Gibey, owned the diner with his wife Elizabeth. Today the diner is owned by Gibey's son Mike and Mike's partner Neil.

3. The Nicest Boiled Dinner Around

IN 1979, AFTER RUNNING THE DINER for almost thirty years, Maurice Wakefield sold the diner to Albert Giberson and his wife Elizabeth. Elizabeth kept the books and Albert, known to all as Gibey, did most of the cooking.

To hear Gibey tell it, he bought the diner on a whim. "I had worked for Metropolitan Life," Gibey says. "One day I was coming out of what used to be Joe's Pizza, and I asked 'How's Maurice doing?' and Joe said 'He wants to sell it (the diner).' So I called Maurice up that night—I mean, there wasn't any pre-planning or anything. Really, I don't think I should have even been in the business, that's how much I knew about it. Maurice gave me a few hints, and showed me how to make biscuits and donuts and muffins and get there at three o'clock in the morning...."

Gibey had learned the basics of cooking from his mother, and between what he already knew, the tips from Maurice, and the diner standards that the staff already knew how to prepare, the diner continued. It was a lot of hard work, with a very small staff.

"I did everything that Mike and the rest of the crew do now," says Gibey. "I'd get up at three o'clock, make donuts, have probably three or four dozen ready to go at five o'clock, and make biscuits and make pies.... I just put it together as I saw it. I took this and that from cookbooks and from the former owners."

Cindy was the mainstay, according to Gibey, along with Bob, whom he affectionately calls "the second owner."

"They did a great job," says Gibey. "They were honest and very willing to do almost anything you wanted them to. Cindy was a worker, boy, she would get up on a step-ladder and wash those ceilings down."

Among the many strange tales from Gibey's time at the diner is the story of how Gibey saved a woman's life. He was working at the diner and someone came in and said there was a woman on the bridge getting ready to jump off. It was a freezing cold November day. "So I walked out there," Gibey says, "and this young lady jumped right off the bridge next to Joe's Pizza. I looked down and said, 'Is anybody helping her?' and they were all just standing around. So I ran around down over the back, and I got in and I pulled her out. She was about ready to go into the heavy current. So I got her out of there. I was just out of breath, and someone else came along and gave me a hand, and then the rescue finally came."

Giberson's Diner, circa 1980. PHOTO COURTESY OF ALBERT GIBERSON

While Gibey claims to have purchased the diner on a whim, he soon became devoted to the task of feeding the town of Gardiner. Like his predecessor, Maurice, Gibey says that meeting people was what he enjoyed most about having the diner.

As in every era of the diner, there were regular customers. "Charlie Merenge and his wife would come every Friday," says Gibey. "They would call ahead and we would have their dinner waiting."

Gibey had a close enough relationship with his regular customers that he got away with teasing them. "I had fun with Charlie," Gibey admits. "He loved chocolate pie, so I went out one time with a plate and a knife and I said, 'Who gave you that big slice of pie? I've got to take half of that away.' I cut it right in two and took it. He said, 'What's this?!'"

No doubt after the joke was over, the rest of the pie was returned.

As in Maurice's day, Gibey's menu kept to a regular schedule. "I'd have beans on Saturday and roast beef on Tuesday. That was always good," says Gibey. "Thursday it was boiled dinner. We had the nicest boiled dinner around. We had people who came in and asked for the boiled dinner. We had baked stuffed fish every Friday. I'd make up a dozen and you thought you were going to run out but you always came out even."

But it was not long after Gibey hit his stride with the diner that the competition increased.

"In the early 1980s it seemed to me everybody was coming into the food business," says Gibey. "When McDonald's came to town, that was like putting a knife in my heart. Breakfast fell off, although we always did a nice breakfast. The people weren't coming any more. They were going out and getting McDonald's sandwiches, or whatever they had for breakfast."

With growing competition and a declining population, the diner business was looking grim. After a few more years of difficult times, Gibey thought seriously about selling the diner. In the mid 1980s he mentioned this to his son Mike, who was then living in Los Angeles.

"Don't do anything," Mike told his father. "I'm coming home."

New England Boiled Dinner

6–8 SERVINGS

Boiled Dinner is one of the traditional dishes that has always been served at the diner. "That was a great thing on a Thursday," says Gibey of this popular menu item. The term New England Boiled Dinner was first seen in print in 1896, and the dish was probably around for at least a century before that.

1 corned beef brisket, 3–4 pounds
5 small onions, peeled and cut in half
8 medium carrots, peeled and cut into large chunks
6 potatoes, peeled and cut in quarters
1 rutabaga or turnip, peeled and cut into large chunks
1 medium head of cabbage, cut in wedges

Place the brisket in a large pot and cover with water. Cover the pot tightly and simmer for about $3^1/2$ hours, or until the meat is tender. Skim off any excess fat.

Add to the pot the onions, carrots, potatoes, and rutabaga. Cover the pot and simmer for another 20 minutes.

Remove the meat to a heated platter and keep warm (cover with foil, or put in a warm oven).

Add the cabbage to the pot and simmer uncovered for 10–15 minutes, until all of the vegetables are tender.

While the vegetables are simmering, slice the meat.

Serve the meat with the vegetables and the liquid from the pot.

In Gibey's day, the boiled dinner was not actually boiled. It was made in an enormous pressure cooker with racks that each held a large pan. First Gibey pressure-cooked the brisket. Then he removed the meat and added the vegetables to the broth left by the meat. When the vegetables were finished, the sliced meat, vegetables, and broth would be combined.

The giant pressure cooker almost exploded one day when the pressure relief valve failed. Sadly, the old machine was beyond repair—the manufacturer had gone out of business, and there were no spare parts available.

Without the pressure cooker, Mike and Neil turned to the traditional boiled dinner, which really is boiled. Or at least simmered.

Salmon Loaf with Egg Sauce

8 SERVINGS

This recipe calls for soft bread crumbs, which are made from fresh bread. At A1 Diner, rye bread crumbs are used in this dish.

1 1/2 pounds fresh salmon, poached
3 cups soft bread crumbs
2 eggs, beaten
3/4 cup half-and-half
1/2 cup shallots, finely chopped
1 cup finely chopped celery
1 cup finely chopped mushrooms
1/4 cup chopped parsley
3 tablespoons butter
2 tablespoons lemon juice
1 tablespoon fresh dill
salt and freshly ground black pepper, to taste

Heat the oven to 350° F. Butter a loaf pan.

Flake the salmon (create bite-sized pieces using a fork; the salmon will naturally fall into flakes).

Mix all ingredients, place in pan, and smooth the top.

Bake for 1 hour or until firm and slightly puffed.

Serve warm, with Egg Sauce if desired.

To poach the salmon, bring to a boil a pan of water, fish broth, or chicken broth large enough to hold your salmon. Add one chopped onion and a handful of parsley stems. If using water, add 2 teaspoons salt. When the liquid is boiling, add the fish, then reduce the heat to a simmer. Cook the fish for 10 minutes per inch of fish. (If the fish is one inch thick, cook for 10 minutes. If it is two inches thick, cook for 20 minutes. If it is 1/2-inch thick, cook for 5 minutes. And so on.)

"10 minutes per inch" is a very useful rule of thumb. Sometimes called the Canadian Fish Rule, it works for every kind of fish and every cooking method (baked, fried, poached, grilled, etc.).

Egg Sauce

This is a classic white sauce, or béchamel, to which hard-boiled eggs are added. At the diner, this has long been the sauce of choice for fish.

6 tablespoons butter
6 tablespoons flour
3 cups milk, heated to very warm
salt and freshly ground black pepper, to taste
6 hard-boiled eggs, sliced

Melt the butter in a heavy saucepan. Add the flour and cook, stirring, over medium heat, for about 2 minutes. Don't let it brown.

Add the warm milk, gradually, and continue to stir as the sauce thickens. Bring the mixture to a boil, then lower the heat and cook, stirring, for about 3 more minutes. Add salt and pepper to taste (start with about $1/2$ teaspoon salt).

Remove from the heat. Add the hard-boiled egg slices.

Serve with the Salmon Loaf.

TWO

The New Kids

1. A Chance to Pursue the Dream

Mike Giberson grew up in Farmingdale, the next town up the Kennebec River from Gardiner. He loved the diner and he loved the soda fountain at Manson & Church's drugstore one door down from the diner, on the corner of Bridge and Water Streets. Mike appreciates longstanding traditions. And he has always been interested in food.

Mike started cooking when he was ten years old. He would cook in secret, when his parents weren't around. If a dish didn't turn out, he would hide the evidence. If it did turn out, he would present it to the family.

Mike's first job as a professional cook was at a home for elderly women in Augusta. These were women who didn't have health issues, so there were no constraints as to the food choices. When Mike took over that kitchen he stopped opening soup cans, as his predecessor had done, and started making fresh food every day. "Those ladies were so happy to have real soup," he remembers. Meeting Mike and hearing him talk about food, one realizes that it's not just food that he loves. He also loves nurturing people.

In 1983, Mike moved to the Boston area for a change of pace and worked as both a cook and a waiter. As a waiter at Legal Sea Foods, he met Neil Anderson, and the two became close.

Neil had also been around food his whole life. His grandparents were caterers, and as a kid he would tag along with his grandmother. "She was a really good cook," says Neil, "she made good homemade basics." Neil worked in many restaurants as a young man, more in "the front of the house" as restaurant people call the non-kitchen part of a restaurant operation, first bussing tables, then working as a waiter and tending bar.

While working together at Legal Sea Foods, Mike and Neil contemplated the idea of opening a little restaurant, maybe a breakfast place. Between them, they had the two sides of the restaurant business covered, the kitchen and the front of the house. But then Mike moved to Los Angeles and the idea was dropped. A few months later, Mike was looking for a reason to leave Los Angeles when his dad mentioned his interest in selling the diner. Here was a chance to pursue the dream that had been deferred.

Mike called Neil and asked if he was still interested in running a restaurant together. He was. In 1985, Mike moved to Gardiner and began working at the diner part-time for his dad, Gibey, to get a sense

Mike and Neil in the early days, when they had first started running the diner. PHOTO BY LYNN KARLIN

of what running the diner entailed. He lived in the apartment downstairs, below the diner's kitchen. Neil moved to Gardiner in 1986. For the next two years, Mike and Neil formulated their vision for the diner, worked on a business plan, and then sought funding.

In addition to a love of food, Mike and Neil share an entrepreneurial drive.

"Part of the motivation was that we had been treated badly enough in enough places by others," says Mike. "After that, if you have the opportunity to not work for someone else, it looks good. Before you realize how much work it is!"

In a certain sense, taking over the diner was easier than opening a new place. Neil says, in retrospect, "I think it was better that we did it here, where we had a little more room to learn and grow and make mistakes. In the city you have to hit the ground running. Here, the expectations probably weren't that high when we took over the diner. So that worked to our advantage."

Expectations may have been low, but the challenge was huge. At this point in its evolution, Gardiner was a dying mill town. Nearly all the mills had gone. The shoe factories had gone. Gibey had been steadily losing customers, both to the newly emerging competition and because of the changing demographics of Gardiner; many of his regular customers had died.

"Gardiner was down to its lowest point," says Danny Chapman, who, along with his brother, owned the service station that was across from the diner until 2005. "There was nothing on the main street. The traffic was just going through."

Mike and Neil knew that to make the diner successful, things would have to change. They would need to attract a younger crowd to stay in business. They had a guiding vision of a high-quality restaurant that would emphasize fresh, local foods and interesting cuisine. Yet their immediate survival required that they keep the existing customers, who counted on the diner for their old favorites. Achieving their vision would require a careful balancing act.

In 1987, Gibey turned most of the day-to-day operations over to Mike and Neil, with the expectation that they would purchase the diner if they could get the funding.

While Mike and Neil had dreams for the diner's future, Gibey had concerns. He wanted Mike and Neil to wear uniforms—"kitchen whites." They refused. He wanted them to keep the food the way it was. They were determined to make changes.

"The inevitable confrontation came over the fish chowder," says Mike. "My dad made it so thick that the spoon stood up in it. I insisted on lightening it up. We got into a big argument. But it wasn't just the chowder, really, it was a culmination of events. It was him letting go, and us needing to assert ourselves."

It was a difficult situation in which to be assertive. The longtime kitchen employees saw themselves as the authorities on how things should be. Points out Mike, "The dishwasher had been here sixteen years, Bob had been here thirty-five years, Cindy for twenty-four. We were the newcomers. Not to mention that we were a couple of gay guys in a small town."

With a clear view of the obstacles before them, Mike and Neil were nevertheless determined to move ahead with their dream. In 1988 the couple proceeded to purchase the diner.

Most customers don't look through this window, but the kitchen staff always looks out.

2. They Worked All the Time

JUST AS MAURICE HAD CHANGED THE NAME to Wakefield's when he purchased Heald's Diner from Eddie Heald, and Gibey had changed it to Giberson's Diner in his day, Mike and Neil changed the name to reflect the new ownership. Neil had given Mike a big neon sign saying A1 for his birthday one year, since Mike loves neon. Inspired by the neon sign, A1 Diner became the name for the new venture.

That was the first of many decisions, and it was probably the easiest one. One of the most difficult was whether and when to become a non-smoking restaurant.

"It was something we wanted to do from the beginning," says Mike, "But we were very, very nervous about it, because we had a lot of smoking customers."

"The first thing we did was have one booth that was non-smoking down at the far end," says Mike. "That was the non-smoking section, which was laughable, because people could sit right next to you and smoke. Then I think we did two booths, and then we did half the diner, but it was still problematic, because it was a small room and you would still smell smoke. Eventually we decided it was ridiculous and we should just go non-smoking."

A1 Diner became a non-smoking restaurant in 1990. It was one of the first restaurants in Maine to do so, and certainly the first diner. Perhaps because diners have long been known as a place one could go for coffee and a cigarette, the decision received a lot of notice. The American Lung Association picked up on the news item and issued a press release.

"A lot of people called when it was in the paper. We got a bunch of phone calls in the first couple of weeks from people saying, 'We wanted to come to your diner and we never have because it's so smoky in there—we're really glad you've gone non-smoking.'"

Once the new policy was in place, Mike and Neil found that they had gained more than they had lost. "A lot of the smokers were really just coffee drinkers, so we weren't losing a lot of revenue," says Mike. Now they had new customers who were coming in for the food.

Today all restaurants in Maine are required to be non-smoking, but at the time it was a bold move. "We were nervous wrecks," says Mike. "It was just like everything else, should I raise the prices or not raise the prices? You never knew if you were doing the right thing."

But they had the right attitude. "They were determined to make it

This same wooden box has been used to store the letters for the menu board since 1946.

work," says Marlena Klassen, who worked as a waitress during the early days of A1 Diner. "They worked all the time," she says of Mike and Neil. "All the time."

Neil learned to cook. "It was all really new for me," he says. "Having worked in restaurants, I had a fair knowledge of food, but it was the line, the short-order, that I had to learn." The worst part was getting up at four in the morning to turn on the deep-fat fryer and start making donuts. "That was a big change. I wasn't used to that. But there was the excitement of a new venture, and that helped. And I was only twenty-five when I moved up here in 1986, so I had that youthful exuberance going for me. That worked in my favor.... I didn't know any better. I don't think I would be able to do it now."

And the cooking was only part of it. "It was amazing how many hours we had to work," says Neil. "Dealing with the equipment, dealing with the staff, all the details. We had to learn what it meant to be a small business owner and a small restaurant owner. There was just so much to learn."

At this point in the evolution of A1 Diner, most of the menu was still made up of the traditional diner dishes. The menu was still on the original menu board above the counter, but gradually, changes were introduced.

"The first changes we made were just switching to better ingredi-

SPECIALS

8 OZ ANGUS SIRLOIN W CHIPOTLE BUTTER	1395
COWBOY BEEF STEW	1275
GREEK BEEF STEW	1225
RUSSIAN VEGETABLE STRUDEL	1095
GREEK SALAD W FRIED CALAMARI	1075
WILD MUSHROOM RAGOUT	1095
FRESH FRIED HADDOCK	1250
MOUSSAKA	1195
2 PORK CHOPS W APPLE CHUTNEY	1350
MANICOTTI W MUSHROOMS & FENNEL	1095
RISOTTO W ASIAN CHICKEN	1250

In addition to the standard menu, A1 Diner features a changing array of specials, usually several soups, a dozen entrees, and a dozen desserts.

ents," says Mike. "Butter for margarine, real half-and-half for the coffee, unbleached flour. And we eliminated the frozen stuff and started making everything from scratch."

Remembers Neil, "We started to filter things in gradually, one thing at a time. But we didn't want to freak anybody out. We still needed to make the food people were expecting, but we figured we could slip a few things in under the radar. We started very gradually to expose them to new foods."

Mike started adding one or two new specials at each meal. One of the first new menu items was Mexican Chicken Pie. "Then there were more things we wanted to do," says Mike. "The menu board got too congested, so the natural step was to go to a printed menu. That freed up the board for soups, specials, and desserts."

It took a while for the new menu items to be appreciated.

"A lot of people don't like changes," says longtime waitress Cindy DeLong. "When Mike took over, he kept a lot of things like the meatloaf, then he added new stuff, and this yuppie stuff—a lot of people just didn't care for it. But others loved it, they would come, so it balanced out, I think. But it took a few years."

They Worked All the Time

Mexican Chicken Pie

TWELVE 12-OUNCE INDIVIDUAL PIES
This dish is similar to a tamale pie and was one of the first specials Mike and Neil added to the diner menu.

For the filling:

1/4 cup vegetable oil
1 cup green onions (scallions), chopped
2 green bell peppers, seeded and chopped
4 fresh jalapeno chili peppers, seeded and chopped (wear rubber gloves)
4 cloves garlic, chopped
1 small can mild green chilies
10 tablespoons chopped parsley
1/2 teaspoon ground cayenne pepper
2 teaspoons ground cumin
1/2 cup flour
3 1/2 cups chicken stock, warm
1 1/4 teaspoons sugar
2 tablespoons lemon juice
1 whole chicken, cooked, meat removed and cut in chunks
1 bunch cilantro, chopped

For the cornmeal crust:

6 cups milk
1 1/2 cups cornmeal
1 teaspoon salt
2 tablespoons butter, melted
3 tablespoons chopped parsley
6 eggs, separated
1/2 cup pumpkin seeds (optional)

In a large skillet over medium heat, heat the oil and cook the green onions, green pepper, jalapeno peppers, and garlic.

When the peppers are soft, about 10 minutes, add the canned chilies, parsley, cayenne, and cumin. Cook for about 5 minutes.

Add the flour and cook for about 2 minutes, stirring.

Slowly add the warm chicken stock, stirring constantly. Reduce the heat to low and cook the mixture for 10 minutes.

Add the sugar and lemon juice. Remove from the heat and add the chicken meat. Sprinkle with the cilantro and set the mixture aside to cool.

Heat the oven to 350° F.

Make the cornmeal crust:

Heat the milk in a heavy saucepan. When the milk is hot, add the cornmeal very gradually, in a trickle, stirring constantly. Cook for 10 to 15 minutes, until the mixture is smooth and thick.

Add the salt, the butter, and the parsley.

Stir in the egg yolks one by one. Remove the cornmeal mixture from the pan and place it in a large bowl. Whisk it a few times to release some of the heat.

Beat the egg whites until they hold soft peaks. Fold the beaten egg whites into the cornmeal mixture (that is, incorporate them carefully by lifting and turning the batter, without beating; a flexible spatula works well for this task).

Fill the individual pie pans with the chicken mixture.

Spread the cornmeal topping over the chicken mixture and top with the pumpkin seeds, if using.

Bake individual pies for about 25 minutes, until the cornmeal crust is browned and the filling is bubbling.

*At A1 Diner, these are served in an oval "boat" that's about 6 inches long and 1^1/$_2$ inches deep. Home cooks may wish to use 12-ounce disposable foil pot-pie pans. Or use whatever size casseroles you have available, including one large one, if you prefer. A larger casserole will take longer to cook.

They Worked All the Time

3. Oh, How She Chuckled at That

JEAN McWILLIAMS and her late partner Karen Mølvig were regular customers when Mike and Neil were just getting a foothold.

"It was so wonderful that you were able to go there and get all these good foods that you couldn't get anywhere else," says Jean. "Once I moved to Gardiner, it became a Friday night ritual. It would be the same people there, all the time. It was so fun, it was just like hanging out with a bunch of friends. People would talk to one another between booths. Sometimes Neil waited tables in those days, and he always wore something outrageous. These days that's less unusual, but in the early 1990s in Gardiner, Maine, Neil stood out. He was quite the daring fashionista."

One of Jean's favorite dishes at A1 Diner is the Shrimp Scampi. "I've tried that so many places, and it's not as good," she says. "I don't bother trying it anywhere else now, because I just know it's not as good as Mike's. That's my standard. Everyone else's is too greasy, or too dry, or the shrimp is overcooked, or there's not enough garlic."

Jean is also a fan of the Lemon Pudding Cake, saying "it just melts in your mouth."

"My comfort food there is mac and cheese," says Jean. "They make a good mac and cheese. It has a great texture. You get a little bubbling-hot crock, not a chunk on your plate. I also love the Creole Beans and Rice. That's a great winter comfort food for me. And among the soups, I love the Hungarian Mushroom Soup. That's so good. It's like hot velvet. I just savor that when I eat it."

One of the delights of the diner for Jean and so many others was the impeccable service and attention to detail from longtime waitress Cindy DeLong. "Cindy knew how you liked your coffee even if you had only been there once," says Jean. Jean dislikes raisins, so Cindy kept a raisin watch and would let her know when the bread pudding had chocolate chips, instead.

Now part of the standard Cindy lore is the Onion Ring Story. When a friend of Jean's, an onion-ring fanatic, sampled A1's onion rings for the first time, she gave them rave reviews. A year later, her friend visited the diner again. Cindy greeted her with: "Sorry, we're out of buttermilk, so there are no onion rings today." Jean's friend was astounded.

Cindy was pleased. "Oh, how she chuckled at that," says Jean. "Cindy knew she had pulled a fast one."

Mike's Shrimp Scampi

6 SERVINGS

When Mike makes this dish he leaves the tails on the shrimp for better appearance, but it is a matter of preference; remove the tails if you like.

1/2 cup olive oil
8 tablespoons butter (1 stick)
2 heads of garlic, separated into cloves, peeled and finely chopped
juice of one lemon (about 3 tablespoons)
2 tablespoons white wine
1/2 teaspoon salt (or to taste)
freshly ground black pepper
36 medium raw shrimp, shelled and deveined
1 pound of angel hair pasta

Bring a large pot of salted water to boil. Reduce the heat to a simmer. Have all ingredients close at hand.

Warm the oil in a large saucepan or skillet, then melt the butter in the oil. Add the garlic and cook briefly, just until fragrant. Add the lemon juice and the white wine, along with the salt and a few grinds of black pepper.

Add the shrimp and cook just until done; the shrimp will curl up and turn pink.

Turn off the heat and cover the shrimp and sauce to keep it warm.

Return the pasta water to a boil, then add the angel hair pasta. Cook just until done (about 3 minutes).

Drain the pasta, divide into bowls, then pour the sauce over the pasta, making sure each serving has 6 shrimp. Serve immediately.

Oh, How She Chuckled at That

Lemon Pudding Cake

ABOUT 8 SERVINGS

You'll fall in love with this dessert. The thin batter separates as it cooks into two distinct layers, a cake-like top and a pudding-like bottom.

6 tablespoons butter, softened
1¹/2 cups sugar
1¹/2 tablespoons grated lemon peel
8 eggs, separated
¹/2 cup + 3 tablespoons fresh lemon juice
6 tablespoons flour
2 cups milk
pinch nutmeg
pinch salt

Heat the oven to 350° F.

Combine the butter and sugar, then add the lemon peel.

Add the egg yolks, one at a time, beating after each addition until smooth.

Stir in the lemon juice, then stir in the flour, milk, and nutmeg.

Beat the egg whites with the salt just until they form soft peaks.

Fold the beaten egg whites into the batter (that is, incorporate them carefully by lifting and turning the batter, without beating; a flexible spatula works well for this task).

Pour the batter into an ungreased 9 x 13-inch pan, or into eight 4-inch ramekins.

Place in a hot water bath (that is, set the pan or the ramekins in a larger pan and add hot water to the larger pan to reach halfway up the sides of the pan or ramekins containing the pudding).

Bake for about 50 minutes, until the top is set and lightly browned.

Serve tepid or cold, with cream or whipped cream if desired.

Hungarian Mushroom Soup

4 SERVINGS

This recipe is from the *The New Moosewood Cookbook* by Mollie Katzen. In the A1 Diner kitchen, Mike uses the recipe from the book's first printing in 1977, which includes a tablespoon of soy sauce in addition to the salt. (If you want to use the soy sauce, add it with the lemon juice.) While this latest version of the recipe indicates that low-fat milk and reduced-fat sour cream can be used, A1 Diner uses whole milk and regular sour cream, which produces a rich, velvety soup.

2 tablespoons butter
2 cups onion, chopped
1 1/2–2 pounds fresh mushrooms, sliced
1 teaspoon salt
2 tablespoons fresh dill
1 tablespoon mild paprika
2 teaspoons fresh lemon juice
3 tablespoons flour
2 cups water
1 cup milk, at room temperature (can be low fat)
freshly ground black pepper to taste
1/2 cup sour cream (can be reduced-fat variety)
finely minced fresh parsley, for the top (optional)

Melt the butter in a kettle or Dutch oven. Add the onions, and cook over medium heat for about five minutes. Add the mushrooms, salt, dill, and paprika. Stir well and cover. Let cook for about 15 more minutes, stirring occasionally. Stir in lemon juice.

Gradually sprinkle in the flour, stirring constantly. Cook and stir another 5 minutes or so over medium-low heat. Add water, cover, and cook about 10 minutes, stirring often.

Stir in the milk; add black pepper to taste. Check to see if it needs more salt and add a little to taste if necessary. Whisk in the sour cream, and heat very gently. Don't boil or cook it after this point. Serve hot, topped with freshly minced parsley if desired.

Oh, How She Chuckled at That

4. I Think About Her Every Day

Mike's best friend, Jacki Davis High, died in 2002. Mike honors her memory with these words.

JACKI WAS MY MUSE. She was my number one fan and my number one supporter. She boosted my self-confidence when I really needed it.

She was a great promoter for me, too. We made her a special card that said, "Enjoy a free cup of coffee from Pigatha." That was the made-up name she used when she pretended she was a restaurant critic—she would go to restaurants and tell them she was a critic for a fictional paper in Santa Barbara, I think she got the name of it from a soap opera. She told people that in her reviews, instead of stars, she used oinks—one, two, or three oinks. Jacki was wild. But those little cards brought us a lot of business in the early years.

I met her in 1990. She was one of those customers who wouldn't go away. I mean that in a nice way. At first she was The Garlic Lady. She always wanted extra garlic, which is easy enough to do. And she wanted garlic in everything. We even created a waffle with garlic—it's a bacon waffle with garlic-infused maple syrup. And it's good.

Jacki was my food muse, too. She had impeccable taste. She was a great, great inspiration to me. She was always clipping recipes for me, showing me cookbooks, telling me about something she had had in Europe. She was always challenging me and pushing my boundaries.

Jacki always said, "Believe in yourself. Go with your convictions. You have the clearest vision, but you doubt yourself. Believe in your dream." She told me that over and over and over again.

Jacki was the guiding spirit behind everything I do. She is still with me, still my guide. I think about her every day.

Crispy Bacon Waffle with Garlic-Infused Maple Syrup

6 WAFFLES

Mike created this unusual recipe for his friend Jacki, also known as The Garlic Lady.

1 1/2 cups + 3 tablespoons flour
1 1/2 tablespoons baking powder
1/2 teaspoon salt
3 eggs, separated
3/4 cup vegetable oil
2 1/2 cups milk
2 slices bacon
1/4 cup maple syrup
3 garlic cloves, peeled and crushed

In a large bowl, combine the flour, baking powder, and salt.

In a medium bowl, beat the egg yolks, then add the vegetable oil and milk.

In a large bowl, beat the egg whites until they hold stiff peaks.

Add the egg-oil-milk mixture to the dry ingredients. Gently fold the beaten egg whites into the batter (that is, incorporate them carefully by lifting and turning the batter, without beating; a flexible spatula works well for this task).

Cook bacon until crispy. Drain and crumble.

Place the garlic in the maple syrup in a large microwavable container. The container needs to be large because the syrup will bubble up and you do not want it to boil over into your microwave. Microwave for about thirty seconds. Remove the garlic by pouring the syrup through a strainer into a small, warmed serving container.

Stir the crumbled bacon into the waffle batter (if some people are having plain waffles, separate out some of the batter before adding the bacon).

Cook the waffles and serve hot with the syrup.

5. There Were Definite Lines Drawn

MIKE AND NEIL'S FIRST MORTGAGE application for the diner was turned down by a local bank. Mike is pretty sure it was because they are gay. "We jumped through every hoop for that bank," says Mike. "We had a good business plan, my dad was going to continue to hold $30,000 of the mortgage, we had a large down payment, and the business had been there since 1946! It hurt when they turned us down, especially since it took them months to do it."

Some of the customers made it an issue as well. "There was a fair amount of innuendo," remembers Marlena. "People would make comments. I remember one guy who would say things like 'Fried Calamari, that's for gay people, isn't it?' And when Mike was around, this guy would just stare at him."

Some of the regular customers stopped coming in, including one of the Chapman brothers who owned the service station across the street. That was a blow to Mike. "Danny Chapman stayed away for almost five years. That was huge," says Mike. "I mean, this was his place. There's a kick mark on the door from when he goes out the door with his coffee every morning; that wear mark is him and only him. It must have killed him not to come here—he went to high school with Cindy. He was part of the diner family."

"We were young then, and not so confident," Mike adds. "So this stuff really bothered me."

Neil remembers it differently. "I don't know that it was so acknowledged," he says. "I don't think there was much in-your-face discrimination. I knew the guys across the street weren't happy with us, though I didn't really care that much. But there was a nagging doubt, 'Would we be busier if we were a straight couple?' For me, that was more the issue. That's what was upsetting. You want to be busy, you want to be successful, and you hope that doesn't hold you back."

After five years, Danny Chapman finally returned to the diner. He says there was no one moment or clear decision, just a sense that it was time to go back. Today he speaks openly about his early attitude toward Mike and Neil's homosexuality. "It was something different that I wasn't used to. In the 1950s and 1960s, there were definite lines drawn," he says. "Definite lines. It was something that wasn't talked about. And to be more open was a challenge to your manhood. We were pretty crude in the beginning—we really were. I guess a whole bunch of emotions were involved—you know, the big male ego...good old redneck boys.... But the main thing was that I just didn't know

Longtime diner customer Danny Chapman.

how to react. I'm a product of society. Maybe I wasn't using my own mind."

His brother Greg had a different attitude, says Danny. "He accepted it from the start. He's the stability of the two of us, the quiet, deliberate one. I'm off the wall. More outgoing, more emotional. But I'm not half as bad as I was years ago."

It's not an issue now, Danny says. "They put out a good product and they have good service and the rest doesn't matter. And it's not really an issue in society now. Is it?"

Bob Newell

Bob Newell has worked at the diner for more than fifty years. He has worked for all four owners, beginning with Eddie Heald in 1952. Bob now makes the biscuits at A1 Diner, for which he is justly famous.

MY MOTHER WAS A GREAT COOK. She was the best cook in Randolph. Her mother was a cook at a hotel up in Auburn. So it kind of runs in the family.

I worked at the Worster House in Hallowell. It was very famous. People used to come from Boston for Sunday dinner there. Beautiful place. There were three dining rooms, the Harris Room, the Colonial Room, and the Sun Porch. And there were private dining rooms, too, for banquets and things like that. Very nice.

I was third cook up there. Mostly the fry cook. We were famous for our lobster casserole. Someone offered Mr. Worster $25,000 for the recipe. He wouldn't give it to them. Well, I was making it! Of course I would never give it to anyone.

I worked for Maurice for twenty-five years. He was a very nice man to work for. His wife was wonderful, too.

I worked out front on the grill. We made typical diner food—hot dogs, hamburgers, cheeseburgers, and meatloaf. We had wonderful meat in those days—baked ham and roast beef. That was very good. We didn't have the variety that there is now—the younger generation wants something different.

In those days we served Jell-O with every meal. Red Jell-O. Strawberry. That's all we ever served. I made it, three gallons of it every day. I said, "Can't we change? Make a different color?" Finally they said okay, make lime.... Well, it didn't go. People wanted the red.

Jim Whalen got the last Jell-O. When we stopped serving it—he got the last one. He always bragged about that.

The old clientele I first waited on here is all gone now. Dead, you know. Of course, I'm not so young. In the afternoon I get pretty tired sometimes. I go home and go to bed. But I love working here with everybody. I don't want to retire. I love my job.

Mike and Neil took me off the grill and made me a prep cook. I liked that! The grill, that's a killer when you get to be my age. I did that for thirty-six years, sixty-two hours a week. That was a long haul.

I make the biscuits now for Mike and Neil. Before that the owners usually made them, or their wives. Maurice made them, and his wife Edith made them. She was a good cook. A great cook.

I make the coleslaw, too. Mike says I make the best.

We took the fried tripe off the menu maybe a year ago. It wasn't really selling. Younger people don't want it. We used to have people who came from Richmond every Friday night for that fried tripe. I don't particularly care for it myself. It looked great on the plate, though, it really did.

We make wonderful soups. I don't make the soup, but they do a good job with that. We make two clam chowders here now, New England and Manhattan. I like them both, but I still like the New England the best.

Mike and Neil worked at Legal Sea Foods in Boston. That's where Julia Child used to go. I guess they waited on her a few times. I met Julia Child and her husband once, down in Wiscasset many years ago. Her husband was a photographer, and he had a showing of his pictures. Of course we all went because of her. And I met her and talked to her. She was very nice to talk to. She was so tall!

I met Andrew Wyeth here. Oh my word. That was three or four years ago. I was all ready to go home, it was about two o'clock, and I was in the kitchen. There was a man waiting near the kitchen to use the bathroom. He was talking to me about, how long has the diner been here, and how long have you been here.... I said, "Where are you from?" and he said Cushing. I said "That's where Andrew Wyeth lives!" He said, "That's my father, he's right out there." I'm a fan of his, so I ran right out to meet him. They were the nicest people you would ever want to meet. Oh my goodness, they were so down-to-earth.

They had the crab cakes. They loved them.

Bob says the secret to tall, fluffy biscuits is to place them close together on the pan.

Biscuits

This biscuit recipe comes directly from the wooden drawer in the table of Bob's workstation in the kitchen of A1 Diner. It is one-fourth the size of the batch Bob makes at the diner. Bob says the most common error when baking biscuits is to place them too far apart on the baking sheet. Placing them close together makes them rise high. Bob can fit thirty biscuits on a cookie sheet—five across by six down.

4³/4 cups flour
2 teaspoons salt
7 teaspoons baking powder
¹/3 cup shortening
2³/4 cups milk
melted butter for top of biscuits (about 3 tablespoons)

Heat the oven to 350° F.

In a standing mixer (or with a pastry blender or two butter knives), mix together the flour, salt, baking powder, and shortening until it is the consistency of cornmeal.

Add the milk and mix briefly, until just combined. The dough will be very sticky.

Spread a lot of flour on your work surface. Scrape the dough onto the flour.

Using a light touch, shape the dough into a rough rectangle about one inch thick.

Cut the dough into rounds using a biscuit cutter (about 2¹/2-inch diameter) or the edge of a water glass.

Place the biscuits close together (they should be touching one another) on a standard-sized rimmed cookie sheet (also known as a jellyroll pan). Brush with melted butter.

Bake for about 20 minutes, until golden brown. Serve hot.

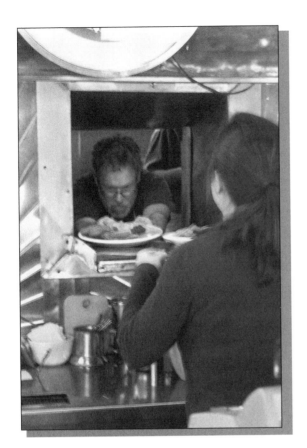 

Left: Maurice Wakefield cut this window between the dining room and the kitchen in the mid 1950s. Right: The diner has long been a favorite for family breakfast.

6. A Reverence for the Place

BENEATH THE DINER'S KITCHEN is an apartment that has housed many a frugal chef and dishwasher, beginning with Maurice Wakefield himself.

One young man who availed himself of the apartment is Brian O'Mahoney, an Irishman who found himself in the improbable situation of living in Gardiner. Stuck in Maine after a failed romance and not finding work after five years of university, he took a job at A1 Diner as a dishwasher and lived for a time downstairs. Proximity made him the go-to guy, so he soon had more shifts than he wanted as washer, waiter, and sometime chef. His parents no doubt thought he had gone mad, but Brian speaks fondly of his time at the diner.

"For me it was like an instant family here," he says. "I was a long way from home and I clearly wasn't thinking very well, but it was fun and interesting and these people were interested in my welfare, for no good reason, just pure kindness. I think it was a great start, a great entrée to American life and society."

Brian speaks of the lore that goes along with the diner, featuring a never-ending cast of characters, "each stranger than the next."

"I think I was lucky to work here when there were a lot of lovely older folks around. When you came here you were sort of expected to learn this cast of characters." Like the mysterious character known as Clyde, who nobody but Cindy could understand. And Jim Whalen, who will be remembered in a section of his own.

Lore was natural to Brian, who had been a history student, so he became a font of diner knowledge. "I went on and learned about the Worcester company," he says, "And what number this is—this is diner number 790, and the Miss Portland is 818, a bit later. There were many diner companies and one of them was O'Mahony, and that's similar to my last name, so that was a nice connection."

Brian says the diner is his favorite building anywhere. "I think it's beautiful," he says. "One of the guys who worked here before me, Ian Inch, had a sort of a love affair with the building as well. He would speak of the way the building was put together, and the wood and steel and Formica, as if he were an architect describing a cathedral."

The building itself and the family atmosphere are two of the aspects of the diner that Brian says give him "an absolute reverence" for the place. A third is the professionalism of the team he was a part of. "Mike and Neil have real attention to detail in the service, which I notice is absent in other restaurants—even very expensive ones," Brian points out. "Like how to put a dessert on the table, or how to hold a glass. You don't hold a glass by the rim. Mike is really big on that."

The first thing Brian learned when he was waiting tables was: No auctioning of food. Brian explains, "That's when you come to the table with the meals and you say, 'Now, Lamb Tagine, who's having that?' Mike and Neil said, 'That's not going to happen here.'" A professional waiter should remember the orders. It's all part of providing an excellent customer experience.

Brian credits Mike and Neil for their vision. "Of all places to have a restaurant, this is not the easiest. If two guys can make a restaurant like this work in a town like this, they can make it anywhere. They have superb taste themselves, and that really makes all the difference. They're not putting it on, they're not looking for someone else's trend, they're actually able to figure out what we want. They have good taste and that leads the way."

Part of the diner lore Brian recounts concerns the window between the kitchen and the seating area. "There's this little tiny window on the world there, and not that many people look into it when they walk in the door, but you always look out," says Brian. One popular kitchen sport is guessing what the patron will order. Does this person look like a meatloaf person? Regular patrons would be tagged with a nickname. The Garlic Lady. Two-biscuit Ned. The Nice Young Couple.

"The Nice Young Couple came here on dates, and then they got engaged, and then they got married," remembers Brian. "And so you watched the progress of people's lives."

"And then I went on to have my progress in life. I got married and had two children, and these guys got to see that. How odd that I would move from Ireland to Gardiner, Maine."

7. Jim, Man of Destiny

JIM WHALEN WAS A FIXTURE AT THE DINER. It seemed he had always been there. He used to say that when the diner was brought to Gardiner on the back of a truck, he was across the street watching with his mom, as he described it, "standing right next to the phone that wasn't there then." He often didn't have water at home, so he relied on the diner, and took all his meals there.

Tori Walsh, who worked as a dishwasher at the diner throughout her high school years, has a vivid recollection of Jim Whalen. "He came in for two or three meals a day. He usually had pie for breakfast. He always carried a big L.L. Bean canvas tote bag with blue stripes. I have no idea what he carried around in there. One time I looked in and I thought I saw kindling." Tori says Jim always wore blue Converse tennis shoes, khaki pants, a navy blue zip-up sweatshirt, and a Greek fisherman's cap. "He would always order two Pepsis. He would tell Cindy, 'I'll have one now and one at the top of the hill.' Because he lived at the top of the hill."

"He was the consummate guy with his ear to the ground in Gardiner," remembers Brian O'Mahoney. "If you wanted to know what was happening, Jim was the guy to talk to."

"He spent $100 a week here, at least, so he settled his bill monthly," remembers Bob Newell. "He liked meatloaf, liver and onions, and pretty much everything—Jim went right through the menu."

Jim had worked for the state making maps, but he was also a painter, as well as a movie buff.

"Jim's stories always followed a certain pattern," says Brian, "Jim encounters authority, authority tells Jim he's wrong, Jim proven right in the end. You know, Jim, Man of Destiny."

A classic Jim Whalen story was the one about the time he and Bob were drafted into the Korean War and went to Portland together. "Jim claimed he wasn't worried at all because he knew he had a condition that would keep him out of the military," says Brian, "but Bob was nervous beyond belief. As the story goes, Bob was so nervous he couldn't eat his breakfast, so Jim ate it for him. And in the end Bob passed the physical and got drafted and Jim didn't. So that was sort of a classic Jim Gets Away with Murder story."

A fresh, hot order of A1 Diner's famous onion rings.

8. Three Whole Minutes

A CHALLENGE FOR THE DINER, and for all restaurants in small towns, is finding staff. "It has always been a challenge and it will always be a challenge," says Mike. "It's just the nature of the business. People come and go. Most people don't choose this as a profession, and those who do gravitate toward the high-end restaurants where the pay is better."

But once in a while, the right person comes along. For about ten years, Chris Breton was the ideal cook for A1 Diner. After that, he moved on to other things, becoming a professional diver. But it was fun while it lasted.

Like most people who work in the A1 kitchen, Chris started as a dishwasher.

"Every dishwasher who walks in that door, once they talk to the other kids, they think they can cook," says Mike. "I tell them first you have to do a good job on the dishes."

Chris did a good job on the dishes, and then he went on to become a good cook.

According to Mike, he was a natural. What makes a good chef? "First it's about liking food," says Mike. "If you don't like food, you shouldn't be in this business. Then there is being a good technician. That's the biggest difference between a good cook and a bad cook. A bad cook agonizes over everything. Even if you follow a recipe, it doesn't come out right if you don't have the touch. It's like Bob with his biscuits—he has the touch. Chris had that. His food always came out great. That used to drive everyone crazy about Chris—he could do it with such ease and have it be good."

The third element, says Mike, is creativity, and that is the element most people lack. A self-taught chef himself, Mike has all three of the necessary elements—love of food, technical skill, and creativity. He shares all these skills freely with his staff, encouraging each trainee to develop his or her own skills and talents. Mike's kitchen is unusual in its flexibility, with team members being cultivated for their personal contributions and abilities rather than being asked to conform to pre-set roles. It's probably the more difficult management choice, but Mike is a natural mentor; he wouldn't be happy if he couldn't give "the kids," as he tends to call them, the chance to grow and learn.

"I didn't start cooking on the line or out back right away," says Chris. "While I was still doing dishes, I started flipping an egg, making a pancake—just doing little things here and there. It takes a while to learn everything, like the order in which things go out. Timing is everything. That part took the longest to learn, the timing."

After about a year and a half, Chris was a diner cook, no longer doing dishes. He was working about thirty hours a week when he was a junior in high school and went full time when he was a senior, as part of a vocational program.

"At that point I actually started going out back," says Chris. "That's what I really wanted to do. They call it prep cook. I enjoyed that because you get to make the food." Chris credits a former diner cook, Julia Cunningham, with teaching him how to make pancakes and eggs, and Mike taught him the rest. "Mike was really kind, really patient," says Chris. "One of the best guys for patience that I ever met—if you messed up, nobody yelled at you, it was just 'Try it again!'"

Ask Chris about his all-time favorites at the diner, and he'll mention a long list of items. Among these is Mike's Bouillabaisse.

But don't get him started on onion rings. "Onion rings, that's one thing I didn't like cooking," says Chris. "Especially when it's busy. You have to cut the onion first, then you have to push the onion rings out into the buttermilk, then fluff them up out of the buttermilk, then drop them into the clam-fry [breading], then mix those up, then put them in the fryolator, and by the time you're done your hands are just coated with this batter, so you've got to wash your hands. The whole process takes, like, three whole minutes to do. So we always hated getting those orders. They loved eating them, though. Mike was always teasing me saying he was going to put a neon sign in the window saying Onion Rings. No! Please, no!"

Bouillabaisse with Rouille

Mike doesn't remember where he first had bouillabaisse, but he absolutely loved it. "After that, I always ordered it, but I was always disappointed," he says. So he decided he would make his own. He calls it the ultimate seafood meal. "It's so satisfying," says Mike, "and it's always a big hit. People seem to think they're getting something really special, although it's just fish stew. But it feels special, and it's as special as what you put in it. It's great with some lobster in the mix."

4 tablespoons olive oil

2 leeks, white and pale-green part only, cut in half lengthwise and then cut in $1/4$-*inch pieces*

2 shallots, minced

6 cloves garlic, minced

1 fennel bulb, cut in half and sliced

1 28-ounce can of diced tomatoes (fire-roasted if you can find them)

1 teaspoon salt

12 cups fish stock or water

grated lemon peel (yellow part only) of 1 lemon

juice of 1 lemon

$1/4$ *cup white wine*

$1/8$–$1/4$ *teaspoon saffron*

freshly ground black pepper to taste

24 fresh mussels and/or fresh clams

2–3 pounds of fish fillets (any firm-fleshed fish such as cod—not delicate fish such as sole)

18 shrimp, raw, peeled, and deveined (the tails are left on at the diner for a nicer appearance; remove them if you prefer)

$1/4$ *cup parsley, chopped*

2 tablespoons Pernod (optional)

Heat a large stockpot on medium heat, then add the olive oil. Add the leeks, shallots, garlic, and fennel and cook, stirring often, for 15–20 minutes, until the vegetables are soft.

Add the diced tomatoes and the salt and continue cooking for 10 more minutes.

Add the stock or water, grated lemon peel, lemon juice, and white wine. Simmer on low heat for 15 minutes.

Add the saffron and pepper. Add the clams, if using, and cook for about two minutes. Then add the mussels, if using, and cook for about two more minutes. Add the fish fillets and cook for about three minutes. Then add the shrimp and cook for about three more minutes.

The goal is to have all the fish done at the same time. The mussels and clams should be just open and the other fish should be just beginning to flake into chunks.

Add the parsley. Add the Pernod, if using.

Serve in wide bowls with a generous dollop of Rouille and lots of crusty bread for soaking up the broth.

⁂ If you can't find saffron you can leave it out and the dish will still be delicious.

⁂ In our recipes in this book, we call for extra-virgin olive oil only when it is important for taste, but Mike uses it for everything, both at the diner and at home. (Some people prefer to use regular olive oil for cooking.) Extra-virgin olive oil is green and fragrant because it comes from the first pressing of the olives. It is much more flavorful than regular olive oil.

Rouille

This is essentially a garlic and red pepper mayonnaise. It adds another dimension to the bouillabaisse.

3 egg yolks
2 tablespoons minced fresh garlic
1 roasted red pepper, seeded, skinned, and cut in strips
1/2 teaspoon salt
1/2 teaspoon freshly ground black pepper
pinch ground cayenne pepper
1 tablespoon lemon juice
1 1/2 cups extra-virgin olive oil

Put all the ingredients except the olive oil in the bowl of a food processor and blend until smooth. With the processor running, drizzle the olive oil into the bowl. Stop and scrape the sides of the processor and pulse once more.

Refrigerate until needed.

You can purchase roasted red peppers, but they don't taste as good as freshly roasted ones.

To roast the red pepper, place it on a pan under a hot broiler and cook for about five minutes, until the skin blackens. Turn it over and continue to roast until the entire skin blackens. Remove from the oven, place in a bowl and cover (or place in a paper bag and close it). After about five minutes, the skin will be loose. Skin, seed, and slice the roasted pepper.

If you would like to keep some roasted red peppers on hand for sandwiches and appetizers, roast several of them as described above, put them in a dish, and cover them with olive oil. They will keep nicely in the refrigerator for about a week.

9. I Don't Know! Cindy Just Brings It

LISA LANE HAS WORKED AT A1 DINER since 1997 and is currently the lead waitress.

"Cindy is my icon," says Lisa. "I told her I want to be like her. I want to stay the course, until my limbs fall off. Actually I think I'm falling apart a lot faster than she did. I don't know how Cindy did it by herself for so long."

Cindy was the only person in recent memory who was able to handle the forty-seat diner all by herself. It took two people to replace her.

The wait staff at the diner does more than just wait tables. Says Lisa, "One of the things about this place is, you're it. If there's a bottle of wine that needs to be opened and served at the table, you're doing it, you're getting it, and you have to know about it. If there's a table that needs to be bussed and rolled over, you're doing it, and then you're hostessing and making sure everyone gets seated. And when it's busy here, there's a line on the sidewalk—it's multi-tasking at its best, let me put it that way."

Cindy's legacy is tough to live up to in more ways than one. Today's staff is at a disadvantage because Cindy had everyone's order memorized. "She never had to ask them the prompt questions," says Lisa, "'What kind of bread do you want, white, wheat, rye, or pumpernickel?' She never had to say, 'Do you want lettuce and tomato?' So when I worked a shift for her, I had to ask the prompt questions, and people would get mad at me! Because they didn't know the answers to the questions any more. They were like, 'I don't know! Cindy just brings it!'"

Even though it has been eighteen years since Mike and Neil took over, Lisa says the transition is still an ongoing process. "There's always an uneducated person who still can walk in that door and be surprised. We still get new customers from people in this area who made a preconceived judgment. Maybe they've heard about the fancy food and they think it's all fancy food. And then they walk in and say, 'I didn't know you had hamburgers and onion rings and meatloaf.'"

According to Lisa, the Greek Salad with Fried Calamari is very popular. "And people love Roger's Chicken Pot Pie. And Roger's pies for dessert. Any pie he makes gets rave reviews."

But Lisa adds, "If Warm Brownie Cup is on the dessert menu, it trumps everything. We have a huge fan base for the brownie cup. People get mad when they come in and it's gone. I tell them they have to come in right when it goes on the menu. This whole diner would be

Lisa Lane, following in the footsteps of Cindy DeLong, now has the preferences of regulars memorized.

storage for brownie cups if we made enough to meet the demand."

Lisa is very clear on her favorite dish. "My favorite, favorite food here is the crab cakes," she says. "Although I really like the Vietnamese Crab Cakes, I LOVE the Maine Crab Cakes. They're a favorite of everybody's. They do not deep fry them, they cook them on the grill. When you get crab cakes here, it's mostly crab. Also there's some corn and sweet red pepper and onion. They're the best crab cakes ever. If I know crab cakes are on the menu, and I have my Monday night off, I'll come in and eat crab cakes and pay full price for them, I don't care. I also love the Chicken Peanut Coconut Curry, but if it's on the menu at the same time as the crab cakes, I'll still get the crab cakes."

I Don't Know! Cindy Just Brings It

Mike's Maine Crab Cakes

12 LARGE CRAB CAKES

Mike is famous for these crab cakes, which are packed full of crab.

1¹/2 pounds fresh crabmeat
1¹/2 cups fresh corn (or frozen corn, thawed)
³/4 cup red bell pepper, chopped
³/4 cup celery, chopped
³/4 cup onion, finely chopped
1¹/2 cups mayonnaise
³/4 teaspoon dry mustard
³/4 teaspoon salt
¹/2 teaspoon freshly ground black pepper
1 egg, beaten
2¹/2 cups saltine cracker crumbs, divided
2 tablespoons butter (or more, if needed, for frying)

Mix all ingredients except the egg, cracker crumbs, and butter.

Gently fold in the beaten egg and 1¹/2 cups cracker crumbs (that is, incorporate them carefully, without beating; a flexible spatula works well for this task).

Place the remaining 1 cup crumbs on a plate or in a shallow dish.

Form the crab mixture into 3-ounce patties (about 3 inches in diameter; or make smaller cakes, if you prefer). Coat the cakes with the cracker crumbs on both sides by placing each cake in the dish of crumbs and pressing gently.

Cook the crab cakes in the butter over medium-high heat until golden brown on each side, about 5 minutes per side.

10. A Place Where They Remember You

BY THE END OF THE 1990s, A1 Diner had achieved a fair amount of recognition. It had been the subject of a positive article in the *New York Times*, been written up in *Down East* and *Yankee* magazines, and was regularly featured in Best Diner coverage nationwide. Many of these mentions are only known to Mike and Neil because of customers, such as the customer from Austin, Texas, who arrived at A1 Diner after reading about the place in his local paper.

"That sort of thing happens a lot," says Mike. "Someone will come in and say 'I sat next to someone on an airplane, and he told me how great your restaurant is, and I finally got to Maine and had to look you up.' I've heard that kind of story a thousand times."

Buffy Parker and Spiros Polemis made their first visit to A1 Diner after reading the 1995 article in the *New York Times*. At the time, the couple lived in Connecticut and were getting ready to move to Maine; they now live in Maine well north of Gardiner, but travel widely in New England, which gives them a chance to frequent A1 Diner. Spiros speaks fondly of the place. "It's the kind of place where they remember you, and you feel welcome," he says. "And of course we love the food. It's exceptional, but not pretentious. It's one of our favorite restaurants in Maine."

As a fan of A1 Diner, Spiros decided to offer Mike a family recipe, a spinach-and-greens pie called Plasto (pronounced Plas-TO) from the Pelion region of Greece. It's rather like the well-known Spanokopita, but with a cornmeal crust rather than the usual filo, and with a mix of greens rather than just spinach. "It's a country dish," says Spiros, "It's meant to be made with whatever you go out and cut from the garden. You could use dandelions, broccoli rabe, or even fiddleheads—whatever is available."

Spiros grew up eating this dish, made by his grandmother, Persephone Voyatzis. When he got interested in cooking as an adult, his grandmother was no longer living and his mother didn't have the recipe. Spiros traveled to Lowell, Massachusetts, the city to which his grandparents and family had originally immigrated from Greece in 1920, and did some detective work to learn more about his mother's family.

At Saint Helen's Greek Orthodox Church, where his grandfather, Aristotle Voyatzis, had been principal of the parochial school, Spiros was referred to two sisters who were childhood friends of his mother, Flo (Florence) and Dickey (Euridice) Houpis. The Houpis sisters

Left: "White, wheat, rye, or pumpernickel?" Right: The original coffee mugs are slightly more shapely than the new ones, but are no longer available. Only the old-timers can tell the difference.

turned out to have the recipe Spiros was seeking. But that is not the end of the tale.

"It tasted great, but there were a few strange things about the recipe," relates Spiros's wife Buffy. "It called for a 500° F oven, which made our whole house fill with smoke. And it called for a whole pound of butter, which seemed like too much."

The couple was friends with a chef, Selma Miriam of the Bloodroot Restaurant in Bridgeport, Connecticut. Selma offered to experiment with the recipe, and she modified it to create the reliable recipe that is in use today in the Parker-Polemis home kitchen, at A1 Diner, and at Bloodroot, where it reportedly sold out every day for a month when it was first placed on the menu.

A Place Where They Remember You

Spiros Polemis's Grandmother's Plasto

10–12 SERVINGS

This recipe was given to Mike by a diner customer, Spiros Polemis, whose grandmother made it for him as a child. Plasto is from the Pelion region of Greece. Use whatever greens you have available; the dish is best with a mixture of greens. (Blanch tough greens in the boiling water, as described for the kale and collards, but not tender greens, such as spinach.) Salty feta is better than mild feta in this dish. Plasto may be eaten warm or at room temperature, and it freezes well. At the diner, this is baked and served in individual casserole dishes.

1 quart milk (4 cups)
12 tablespoons butter (1 1/2 sticks)
1/2 teaspoon salt
1 1/4 cups cornmeal
2 pounds tender greens, such as spinach and escarole
1 pound tough greens, such as collards and kale
3 tablespoons olive oil, plus extra for the crust
1 1/2 pounds feta cheese
5 eggs, beaten well
whole-milk yogurt, as topping (if desired)

Heat the oven to 350° F.

Place the milk, the butter, and the salt in a pot over medium heat and bring to a simmer. Sprinkle the cornmeal into the liquid and stir vigorously, cooking until thickened. The consistency should be like a cooked cereal, neither thick and pasty nor very creamy. Add more milk or more cornmeal if necessary to adjust the texture. Remove from the heat and set aside to cool.

Bring a pot of water to a boil.

Meanwhile, wash and chop the tender greens and set aside. (If using chard, remove and discard the stems.)

Wash the tough greens, remove and discard the stems, and chop coarsely. Add these tough greens (but not the tender greens) to the boiling water. Let boil for 1 minute, then turn out into a colander to drain. Squeeze the moisture out of the greens with your hands, using a towel if necessary. It is important to remove as much moisture as possible, or it will make the bottom crust soggy.

Heat the olive oil in a large frying pan. Add the wrung-out collards and kale (or other tough greens) and cook over medium heat until they begin to brown at the edges, about 10 minutes. Add the tender greens and cook another 10–15 minutes, adding more oil if needed, until all the greens are fully cooked. Set the greens aside to cool. Squeeze them and pour off any moisture remaining.

Crumble the feta cheese with your hands into a large bowl.

Add the beaten eggs and the cooled greens and mix all together.

Spread the cornmeal mixture thinly in a 16 x 12 x 1-inch ungreased pan, or into individual casserole dishes. The cornmeal should not be more than $3/8$-inch thick. Top with the egg-cheese-greens mixture. Spread a thin layer of cornmeal mixture over the top. Sprinkle or brush lightly with olive oil.

Bake 1 hour or until lightly browned on top.

Serve with a large dollop of plain whole-milk yogurt on top, if desired. The cold yogurt is a nice contrast to the hot Plasto.

A Place Where They Remember You

Roger Erickson makes the pies.

11. I Guess We Know Who'll Be Making the Pies

THE PIE MAN, ROGER ERICKSON, has worked at A1 Diner since 1995. He spent time on the grill and as a prep cook before he came to specialize in pies. Working at A1 Diner opened his eyes to the world of food. Says Roger, "When I first came here for breakfast, I looked at the specials and I saw things like Jambalaya and Quesadilla and I thought, this must be a joke! I never heard of food like that! When I started working here and realized that's what I would be making and serving, I thought, *But I can't even pronounce it!*"

"I only knew about traditional food," says Roger. "But it was so much fun to learn about, you know, portobellos, things like that. And about real ingredients, cooking things from scratch. Where I worked before, everything was out of a box. I love the way the food here is made all from scratch. You don't find that a lot."

In the diner kitchen, everyone has a regular spot. Roger and Bob work side by side on the other side of the work table from Mike. The two are very close. "Bob is the best part of working here," says Roger. "I couldn't imagine not having Bob here. He's the one who makes you feel better if you're upset. And he is so funny."

Roger points out that the A1 crew gets along better than many. "In a lot of restaurants, they pit the kitchen against the wait staff," he says. "Very few restaurants, you'll find, do they work together. Here we really try to."

Mike and Neil learned about the negative side of restaurant management when they worked as waiters. "In a lot of big restaurants, common hatred of the owner is what bonds the staff," says Mike. "I worked at one place as a waiter where the owners had the attitude about the staff, 'Never give them what they want, or they'll expect more.' If you wanted Thursday off, they would make sure to schedule you for Thursday. We have the opposite style here. I try to be as supportive and flexible as I can. I only get upset with someone if they're not doing their job."

Roger has had similar experiences. "I try to explain to people," says Roger, "I've worked in different places, and you're not going to find a place that's like this, where they take into consideration your personality. Here, if they like you and they know you're going to work and fit in, they don't want to hassle you. They work with you on the schedules, on your strong points and weak points."

Autonomy is something Mike values and promotes. Says Roger, "Mike really likes it when you get to a point when you can think for

Roger the Pie Man uses small cookie cutters or a sharp knife to make the designs for his crusts.

yourself, get a little more creative, and work on your own. And it's not just so you don't bug him, it's because that's when you come up with the best recipes."

Roger enjoyed being a line cook, but a neck injury keeps him away from the grill. Now he focuses on the pies, a specialty which started when he entered a pie-baking contest at Old Hallowell Days, a summer celebration in a nearby town.

"I made a raspberry pie," says Roger, "and it won first prize. I thought, *I can't wait to tell Michael!* I told him I won the pie-baking contest and he said 'Really! Well, I guess we know who'll be making the pies!'"

Roger's Pie Crust

This is the pie crust Roger uses for all his pies. Make sure the cold ingredients are very cold, and work quickly to keep them from warming up as you mix them. Roger uses unbleached flour.

2 1/2 cups flour
1 1/2 cups sugar
dash salt
16 tablespoons COLD butter (2 sticks)
1/4 cup COLD water

Mix flour, sugar, and salt.

Add the butter and crumble with two forks, a pastry cutter, or your hands. Work quickly to crumble the ingredients together while they are still cold.

When the mixture is crumbled coarsely, add the water just a little at a time until it holds together and forms a dough.

Roll out the pie crust and proceed as directed in the filling recipe.

Roger claims that pie crust is no big deal. He says, "It should not be too sticky, or it won't roll out—but not too dry or it won't hold together. Don't be afraid to add a little extra flour if it's sticky, or water if it's dry. But don't overwork the dough or it will turn out tough. It's best not to think about it—mix, roll, and fill!"

Roger's Award-Winning Raspberry Pie

9-INCH PIE

This is the pie that won Roger first place at the Old Hallowell Days pie-baking contest. It was inspired by the raspberry pies of a family friend known as Aunt Frances, who is from Hallowell. Use a full cup of sugar for a sweet pie, 3/4 cup sugar for a pie that is more tart. Taste the filling to be sure, since some raspberries are sweeter than others.

1 pint fresh or frozen raspberries
between 3/4 and 1 cup sugar (to your preference)
if using frozen berries, 1 teaspoon tapioca
dash salt
squirt lemon juice
dash cinnamon
pie crust for a two-crust pie
egg wash (one egg beaten with 3 tablespoons milk, for coating pie crust)

Heat the oven to 350° F.

If using frozen berries, put them in a bowl, add the tapioca and the sugar, and let the berries thaw. If using fresh berries, put them in a bowl, add the sugar, and let stand for a few minutes.

After the fresh berries have set for a few minutes, or after the frozen berries have thawed, add the salt, lemon juice, and cinnamon.

Place one crust in the pie plate, fill the pie, and cover with the top crust. Trim the edges to within about one inch of the pie plate, then fold the top crust under the edge of the bottom crust. Crimp the edge in a fluted pattern with your fingers, or flatten it with a fork.

Brush the top crust with the egg wash to help make it crisp and give it a golden brown color when baked. Make a hole in the center, or cut the crust in a few places, to allow the steam to escape.

Bake the pie for 30 minutes, until the filling is bubbling and the crust is light golden brown.

In general, Roger likes to use tapioca to thicken his pies. He finds it interferes less with the flavor than flour does. When using fresh raspberries for this pie, the tapioca isn't needed because of the natural pectin in the fresh fruit.

Roger's Apple Pie

9-INCH PIE

Apple pie is a favorite at the diner. Roger also makes small, individual-sized versions of his fruit pies for A1 To Go.

8 cups apples, cored, peeled, and sliced
1 cup sugar
1¹/2 teaspoons cinnamon
¹/2 teaspoon nutmeg
¹/2 teaspoon ginger
dash salt
2 teaspoons lemon juice
3 tablespoons butter, melted
2 teaspoons tapioca
pie crust for a two-crust pie
egg wash (one egg beaten with 3 tablespoons milk, for coating pie crust)

Mix all ingredients (except for the egg wash) and allow the mixture to sit at least 20 minutes.

Heat the oven to 350° F.

Fit the bottom crust into the pan. Fill the pie with the apple mixture, then top with the second layer of pastry. Trim the edges to within about one inch of the pie plate, then fold the top crust under the edge of the bottom crust. Crimp the edge in a fluted pattern with your fingers, or flatten it with a fork.

Brush the top crust with the egg wash. Make a hole in the center, or cut the crust in a few places, to allow the steam to escape.

Bake for about 40 minutes, until the apples are soft and the crust is browned.

Roger's Chicken Pot Pie

After trying many recipes for chicken pot pie and never finding one they thought was good enough, Mike and Roger created this recipe, which seems to be perfect. At the diner this is served in individual casserole dishes. Disposable foil pans, available widely, are very handy. If you prefer, you can make two 9-inch pies, or the equivalent number of odd-sized pies.

1 small chicken (about 3 pounds)
3 tablespoons olive oil
3 onions, chopped
4 tablespoons minced garlic
9 ribs celery, cut into ¹/4-inch dice
8 carrots, cut into ¹/4-inch dice
1 teaspoon ground dried thyme
¹/2 teaspoon ground dried sage
4 tablespoons fresh rosemary leaves, finely chopped
2 cups fresh corn kernels or thawed frozen corn
1 cup frozen peas, thawed
10 tablespoons (1¹/4 sticks) butter
1 cup flour
6 cups chicken stock, boiling
2 cups half-and-half
salt to taste
freshly ground black pepper to taste
pie crust for a two-crust pie
1 egg
2 tablespoons half-and-half

Poach the chicken in a large pot of gently boiling water until it is just cooked. Drain and set aside. When the chicken is cool, pull off all the meat and chop it into bite-sized chunks.

Heat the oil in a medium-sized pan. Add the onion and cook over medium heat for 10 minutes.

Add the garlic, celery, and carrots and cook until the vegetables are tender, about another 10 minutes.

Add the herbs and cook for 3 minutes more.

Remove the pan from the heat and add the corn and the peas.

Melt the butter in a medium-sized pan over medium heat.

Add the flour and cook, stirring, until it is well incorporated with the butter, about 5 minutes. Do not let the mixture brown.

Add the boiling chicken stock, stirring constantly as the mixture thickens.

When the sauce has thickened, about 5 minutes, add the half-and-half. Season to taste with salt and pepper.

In a large bowl, combine the vegetable mixture, the sauce, and the chicken. Mix together, then fill the individual casseroles and set aside while you prepare the pastry.

Heat the oven to 350° F.

Roll out the pie crust to 1/4-inch thick, cut it to fit your casseroles, and place a crust on each filled casserole.

Whisk together the egg and the half-and-half, then brush some of this mixture over each sheet of pastry. (This egg wash helps the pastry to brown.)

Bake for 30 minutes.

I Guess We Know Who'll Be Making the Pies

Hazel Newell's Squash Custard Pie

9-INCH PIE

Hazel Newell was Bob Newell's mother—reportedly the best cook in Randolph, Maine. Bob always liked this pie of his mom's and asked Mike if they could serve it at the diner. No one seemed to have the recipe, so Mike recreated it based on Bob's recollections. The pie is unusual in that it separates during cooking into a squash layer and a custard layer.

5 eggs
1 cup white sugar
1 cup canned squash puree (fresh squash has too much moisture)
1 cup milk
2 cups heavy cream
1 teaspoon vanilla
1 9-inch pie shell, uncooked (bottom only)

Heat the oven to 350° F.

In a medium-sized mixing bowl, combine the eggs and the sugar with a whisk. Add the squash, the milk, the cream, and the vanilla, and mix, but do not beat.

Pour into the large pie shell and bake for 50–60 minutes until just set. Chill before serving.

THREE

⁂

Main Street Maine

1. Alimentari = Al To Go

THE YEAR WAS 2002. For over a decade, Mike and Neil had not only kept the diner alive, but created an interesting new restaurant that preserved the best of its past while embracing the best of the present. They had created a successful small business, earned the respect of the community, and achieved their dream.

But the dream, as dreams do, expanded.

It was their first visit to Italy, and Mike and Neil were entranced by the hill towns of Tuscany—the architecture, the style, the tradition, the lovely plazas and courtyards, and of course, the food. "I remember one plaza in particular that has a triangular shaped center," says Neil. "It's lined with cheese shops and shops with all the prosciuttos hanging in them... these food shops were so beautiful and the food looked so great, we thought, 'Wouldn't it be wonderful to do that?'"

So the seeds were sown for a new venture: a community market and café that would provide beautiful food for the people of Gardiner.

Some felt it would be a huge risk. Was Gardiner ready for an upscale market? Did it make sense to put another café right next to the diner?

But Mike and Neil had a sense that the time was right.

"There were similar things happening in other parts of Maine," says Neil. "There was Treats, in Wiscasset, which Michael was very fond of, and our friends had Aurora Provisions in Portland, and that was very successful. So we said, 'Well, why *can't* this succeed here? There's really nothing close by.'"

Shortly after Mike and Neil returned from Italy, they learned that an old building around the corner from the diner was about to be renovated. The Manson & Church Building, as it is still known, takes that name from the drugstore it housed for many years, which once had an old-fashioned soda fountain; Mike has fond memories of going there as a kid. The building is in a prominent location at the corner of Bridge Street and Water Street, Gardiner's main street. In Gardiner's glory days it was a beautiful landmark building, but for the past few years it had been vacant, an eyesore that provided a daily reminder of Gardiner's decline. Local small business owners Jeff and Eva Cole were looking for a site for a new business, and they decided to renovate the building.

"When Jeff and Eva took this building over and renovated it, things just all kind of fell into place," says Neil. Jeff and Eva's business was on the second floor, so the first floor became available. It was an

A1 To Go features a stylish, contemporary look.

ideal location for the community market. Says Neil, "Michael just jumped on it, because he knew. Having it right next to the diner, and being on the corner, and having all these windows, it seemed serendipitous."

Things were beginning to look up in Gardiner. A hard-working cadre of local businesspeople had been working to revitalize the local economy as part of the statewide Main Street Maine program, administered by the Maine Downtown Center (part of the Maine Development Foundation, a non-profit firm that works closely with government but is largely funded by private enterprise). Gardiner was chosen in 2001 to be one of the first Main Street Maine communities, and the town's Gardiner Main Street organization has made the program a smashing success.

Mike has been a very active member of the Gardiner Main Street program, chairing its design committee and now serving as the president of the board of directors. In 2005 Mike received the Maine Downtown Center award for Volunteer of the Year.

Mike is impressed with the program's effectiveness. "There have been many previous attempts to revitalize the downtown area, but they never worked because you can't just throw money at the problem," says Mike. Unlike previous efforts, Main Street Maine is a structured, incremental program that addresses every aspect of revitalization, from economic restructuring to good design. The program is locally owned and operated, and is funded by the city and its merchants, creating a true commitment.

"There has been a world of difference in Gardiner since the Main Street program came into existence," says Mike.

Among the visible differences are the new businesses in downtown Gardiner. Over two dozen new firms have come to downtown Gardiner since the Main Street Maine program was initiated, among them the companion retail store to A1 Diner, A1 To Go.

"Before we had the store, we felt we weren't really part of downtown," says Mike. "We were around the corner, on the bridge; we were different, in more ways than one. People would say to me, 'You have your own little world here. You're the only thing going on in this town.' We heard this over and over again. When we moved into the store, that made us part of 'Main Street.' Being right on the corner in this beautiful old building, we now feel like we're really part of things."

Neil points out that the variety of offerings is part of what makes A1 To Go successful. The café serves excellent sandwiches to eat in or take out. Prepared entrées are available to go for the after-work crowd, and a catering business has started to grow by popular demand. Matt Rowe's Korean specialties sell very well. The A1 To Go espresso bar does a brisk coffee business at breakfast, and a nice assortment of baked goods is a natural complement. Danielle Doyon, A1's pastry chef, creates delicious works of art, and Mike has been having fun lately as the Cookie King with his infinite variations on popular cookies, always oversized. Roger makes small pies for A1 To Go, just right for one or two portions, and the store also sells artisan breads from nearby bakeries. The center aisles are taken up with a gourmet food section, and the dairy case offers special cheeses along with chilled wine and beer.

"Someone comes in for a loaf of bread, and they pick up a bottle of wine to have with dinner, and then maybe they get a cookie to have with a cup of coffee," says Neil. "I wouldn't want to rely on any one of those. It would be much harder to be just a coffee shop, or just a wine store. This way, all the parts complement each other. It makes for a more interesting experience for the customer, too. It gives them inspi-

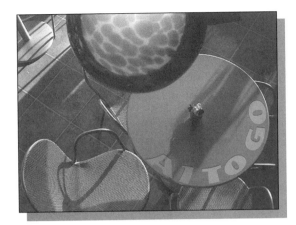

Top left: A view of the seating area.
Bottom left: Great meals to take home.
Above: Matt Rowe makes the sushi.

ration. Michael has done a great job stocking the shelves, finding things people want."

Another contribution A1 To Go makes to Gardiner is its lovely atmosphere. The overall impression is one of calm and elegance. The large room has a bright, airy feeling, with high ceilings and lots of natural light. There are several tables and chairs in the front of the room, where the light is most plentiful—it's an inviting place for a meeting over coffee or lunch. A floor-to-ceiling wine rack filled with outstanding selections adds visual interest. Even the gourmet food items on the shelves in the center of the store have a tendency to be beautiful.

"The atmosphere is a big part of it," says Neil. "The colors are really right. The big windows are so nice. We have interesting lighting. I think it's fairly contemporary for this area, but people respond to it. It's not overly challenging. It's unusual but comfortable."

It's a perfect space for monthly wine tastings and community

Neil pours a taste at one of A1 To Go's popular wine tastings.

events. Neil is particularly proud of the 2005 poetry reading by Baron
Wormser, then Maine's poet laureate.

Events have helped spread the word about A1 To Go, and business
is growing. Mike and Neil are realistic about what it takes to attract
business to a new enterprise in a small town. "People need to hear
from others," says Neil. "I think around here people wait a year and
then if you're still around they'll try it."

Early on in their planning for A1 To Go, Mike and Neil struggled
to find the right name. They wanted it to reflect their vision for the
venture. Since that vision was born in the small traditional markets of
Italy, the name that felt right to Mike was Alimentari, the Italian word
for a small grocery store. To him, the sound of the word evoked everything that inspired the expansion of the dream. But he knew it wasn't
quite right for Gardiner, so he took the practical approach and named
it A1 To Go Community Market and Café.

And yet when one visits A1 To Go, with its bustling, pretty atmosphere, its gourmet delights, and its fine wines and fine food, one feels
that while the name Alimentari might not have been accepted, its spirit
certainly has.

Alimentari = A1 To Go

Curried Chicken Salad

This chicken salad is a favorite at A1 To Go. Mike prefers slivered almonds over sliced almonds, because they "have a better presence"—they don't get lost among the other ingredients. At A1 To Go this chicken salad is usually offered in a wrap. You may wish to follow suit, using a large flour tortilla or lavash bread. Or serve the chicken salad on your favorite bread, or on a bed of lettuce.

6 boneless chicken breast halves
about 1 tablespoon olive oil
3/4 cup best-quality mayonnaise
2 tablespoons curry powder (or more, to taste)
1/3 cup green onions, chopped or thinly sliced
1/3 cup raisins
1/3 cup toasted slivered almonds

Heat the oven to 350° F.

Place the chicken breasts on a baking sheet, coat them lightly with olive oil, then place in the oven. Roast for 16 minutes, then turn the breasts and roast for another 16 minutes or until done (when done, the chicken will no longer be pink).

Let the meat cool, then chop or shred (depending on your preference).

Mix the curry powder into the mayonnaise, then mix the curried mayonnaise with the chicken, then add the rest of the ingredients and mix well.

※ To toast the nuts, bake in one layer on a cookie sheet in the oven at 350° F for about five minutes, until they are slightly browned and taste toasty. Nuts are almost always better toasted.

Mango Macadamia White Chocolate Chip Cookies

1 DOZEN VERY LARGE COOKIES, or 2 dozen regular-size cookies
If you prefer chewy cookies, bake them only until slightly brown. If
you prefer crispy cookies, bake them until they are deep golden brown.

16 tablespoons butter (2 sticks), softened
2/3 cup sugar
3/4 cup brown sugar
2 eggs
1 teaspoon vanilla
2 1/4 cups flour
1 teaspoon baking soda
1 teaspoon salt (use this amount if you are using unsalted butter, as Mike does;
    if you are using salted butter, add only 1/2 teaspoon salt)
2 cups white chocolate chips
1 cup slivered almonds
1 cup dried mango bits

Heat the oven to 350° F.
    Combine the butter and the sugars; beat until smooth.
    Add the eggs and the vanilla, then beat again until smooth.
    Add the flour, baking soda, and salt, and mix until just combined.
    Stir in the chips, almonds, and mango bits.
    Drop the dough onto a silicone baking mat such as Silpat, placed
on top of a cookie sheet. (Or use a greased cookie sheet, but be careful
not to let the cookies get too dark on the bottom.) Flatten slightly and
shape into rounds. If you are making large cookies, use all the dough
to make one dozen. If you are making smaller cookies, use half of the
dough and then use the rest to make a second dozen.
    Bake 20–25 minutes, depending on whether you want the finished
product to be chewy or crispy. Turn the cookie sheets after ten minutes
to promote even baking.
    Cool the cookies on a wire rack.

Lime Avocado Salad with Pistachios

ABOUT 6 SERVINGS

Mike invented this salad for A1 To Go, where it has been wildly popular. "Everyone loves this," says Mike. It's a nice dish to serve in warm weather.

3 perfectly ripe avocados, cut into bite-sized chunks
1/2 red onion, chopped
1/4 cup fresh lime juice
1 small sweet red pepper, chopped
1/3 cup chopped fresh cilantro (about 1/4 bunch)
1/8 cup chopped crystallized ginger
1 jalapeno pepper, seeded and chopped (use rubber gloves)
1 tablespoon vegetable oil
1/4 teaspoon salt
1/4 teaspoon freshly ground black pepper
1/4-inch piece of fresh ginger, peeled and minced
1/2 pint grape tomatoes (or use cherry tomatoes)
1/2 cup chopped pistachios

Mix all ingredients, except the pistachios, in the order given. Sprinkle the pistachios on top.

Fresh ginger is very stringy. To mince it successfully, first cut the peeled ginger into coins, then mince the coins. Cutting it crosswise into coins severs the stringy fibers, which run the length of the ginger root.

Chap Chae (Korean noodles with vegetables)

6 SERVINGS

This recipe is from Matt Rowe. Matt sells his Korean food through A1 To Go, which also carries his sushi. "Matt's food is a dynamic part of the case," says Mike. In other words, they sell a lot of it.

1 onion
1 carrot
1 red pepper
4 ounces mushrooms
4 green onions (scallions)
1 10-ounce package bean thread noodles
1/2 cup sugar
2 tablespoons sesame oil
2 tablespoons finely minced garlic
pinch ground cayenne pepper
1/4 cup soy sauce
2 tablespoons vegetable oil

Cut the onion, the carrot, and the red pepper into small pieces the size and shape of matchsticks. Slice the mushrooms. Cut the green onions into one-inch pieces, on the diagonal.

Soak the noodles in hot water until they are soft, then drain and rinse.

In a small bowl, make the sauce: first combine the sugar, sesame oil, garlic, and cayenne, then add the soy sauce.

In a medium skillet over medium heat, cook the onion, carrot, red pepper, and mushrooms in the vegetable oil for about 10 minutes until they begin to soften.

Add the sauce to the pan, stir, then add the noodles. Cook for another 7 minutes, then drain excess liquid and serve.

Add the raw green onions to the finished dish as a garnish.

2. A Very Special Dinner

GREAT CHEFS ARE OFTEN KNOWN for their ability to pair wine and food. A variation on that theme is the dinner Mike created in 2005 that paired foods with some interesting beers.

The Quebec-based microbrewery, Unibroue, is known for its bottle-fermented Belgian-style ale. The natural carbonation that results from its bottle fermentation gives these beers a characteristic mouth feel that makes them ideal beverages to enjoy with a meal. "People are often surprised that beer can go with a fine meal," says the firm's New England regional manager, Richard DelMonico, "but Belgian-style ales pair very, very well with food."

For the beer dinner, Mike created three special dishes and A1 pastry chef Danielle Doyan created a dessert. DelMonico says the pairings of these dishes with his beers were among the best he has experienced.

A1 Diner is a cozy venue for special events.

Warm Lentil Salad with Poached Egg

4 SERVINGS

In the winter and spring of 2004, Mike took two trips to Paris. "The food was superb," he says. "In a café on the Champs Elysées, I had a wonderful lunch and I tried to recreate part of it with this Warm Lentil Salad. It makes a great start to a meal or with a couple of poached eggs it can be a meal in itself."

At the beer dinner, this course was served with Unibroue's Blanche de Chambly White Ale, which has a hint of citrus, a classic flavor element in Belgian white ales. The citrus flavor matches well with the lentils, and the mild flavors of the beer suit the mild flavors of the dish.

1¹/2 cups dry lentils, rinsed
6 cups water
1 large leek, white and light-green part only, chopped and washed
1 carrot, peeled and finely chopped
2 celery stalks, finely chopped
1 tablespoon extra-virgin olive oil
2 teaspoons fresh thyme leaves
1 tablespoon parsley, chopped
salt
freshly ground black pepper
4 poached eggs

Place the lentils in a medium saucepan and cover with water. Bring to a boil, then reduce the heat to a low boil and cook for 20 to 25 minutes. The lentils should be tender but not mushy when done.

While the lentils are cooking, cook the vegetables: in a large skillet or medium saucepan, cook the leek, carrot, and celery in the olive oil over medium-low heat until soft, about 20 minutes.

Add the thyme, parsley, and salt and pepper to taste.

Drain the lentils, keeping one cup of the cooking liquid. Add the lentils to the vegetables. If you want a little sauce, add up to 1 cup of the reserved cooking liquid.

Season with more salt and pepper to suit your taste.

Top with the poached eggs and garnish with chopped parsley.

⚜ Leeks often contain a fair amount of sand in their tightly furled leaves. Mike overcomes this problem by chopping the leeks first, then washing the chopped leeks in a colander.

Penne Arrabbiata with Crispy Pancetta

4 SERVINGS

"I love fiery tomato sauce," says Mike. Arrabbiata means "angry" in Italian, and is often used to denote spicy dishes, the way "deviled" dishes are spicy in American home cooking.

At the beer dinner, this was served with Unibroue's Maudite, a Strong Red Ale, which has a complex flavor profile. The ale has a spicy flavor to match the spicy pasta, along with a sweet flavor that goes with the pancetta. The beer also has some lingering bitterness of hops, which works well with the spiciness of the dish.

This dish is also great with a hearty red wine.

1/4 cup extra-virgin olive oil
3/4 teaspoon hot red pepper flakes
4 shallots, peeled and chopped
3 garlic cloves, peeled
3 anchovies, rinsed and chopped with the garlic
1 teaspoon salt
1 28-ounce can diced tomatoes (fire-roasted if you can find them)
1 15-ounce can tomato sauce
1/4 cup finest-quality tomato paste
1 bunch fresh oregano, chopped coarsely and divided
1 pound penne or other pasta
12 slices pancetta, chopped
1 cup grated Grana Padano or Parmigiano-Reggiano cheese

Have all of your ingredients prepped and ready.

Heat a large, heavy saucepan over medium heat. Add the olive oil to the hot pan and toss in the red pepper flakes. Let them cook for just a few seconds—you want to infuse the oil with the fiery heat of the flakes, but you do not want to burn them.

After the pepper flakes have cooked a few seconds, add the shallots, garlic, anchovies, and salt. Cook over medium-low heat for 20 minutes, stirring frequently.

Add the tomatoes, tomato sauce, tomato paste, and half of the oregano, and turn the heat down to low. Cook, covered, for 45 minutes.

Add the rest of the oregano. Keep the sauce warm while you cook the pasta.

Cook the pasta in plenty of boiling water, then drain.

While the pasta is cooking, cook the pancetta in a skillet over high heat until it is crispy, about 10 minutes. Drain it on paper towels.

Divide the pasta into 4 bowls and add a generous amount of sauce. Top with grated cheese and garnish with the crispy pancetta.

Pancetta is an Italian cured meat similar to unsmoked bacon. Bacon is an acceptable substitute.

Mike always uses anchovies when making any kind of marinara (tomato-based sauce for pasta). If you think you don't like anchovies, you may leave them out, but even the anchovy-phobic often find that they appreciate the flavor of this sauce when it is complete.

Spiced Brisket with Soft Polenta

8–10 SERVINGS

Mike's inspiration for this dish was a meal he had in Paris: "Sans the chipotle, but that's my little twist. It was a fabulous lunch in the shadow of the Arc de Triomphe. I dined at the bar with a Parisian lawyer born in Haiti. He was as delightful as the meal and the first Parisian I had a real conversation with."

At the beer dinner, this dish was served with Unibroue's La Fin du Monde Golden Ale, which has a strong and spicy flavor, along with a bit of tartness. The flavors match nicely with the flavors of the spicy brisket, and the champagne-like effervescence of the beer cleanses the palate.

For the brisket:

4 to 5 pounds beef brisket, fat left on (don't let the butcher trim the cap)
1/3 cup brown sugar
2 tablespoons salt
2 tablespoons freshly ground black pepper
1/3 cup chipotle in adobo sauce, mashed with a fork or pureed in a blender
1 teaspoon ground cumin
1 teaspoon allspice
1/2 teaspoon cinnamon

Heat oven to 250° F.

Mix all spice ingredients and rub on the brisket.

Put the brisket, fat side up, in a baking dish with a tight-fitting lid. (If you don't have a dish with a tight-fitting lid, place a piece of foil over the pan and then add the lid.) The tight-fitting lid is important—otherwise the meat will dry out.

Bake for 2 hours, then increase the oven temperature to 350° F. Bake for another 2 1/2 hours, then cut into the meat to check for tenderness. If it is not quite tender, cook for another half hour.

When the brisket is tender, place it on a cutting board and slice.

Serve the slices on soft, creamy polenta.

For the polenta:

1 cup cornmeal
5 cups water
2 teaspoons salt
1/2 teaspoon freshly ground black pepper

In a heavy saucepan, bring the water to a boil.

While whisking, add the cornmeal in a steady stream.

Continue whisking in the same direction until the polenta is creamy.

Reduce the heat to a bare simmer and cook, whisking occasionally, for 15 to 20 minutes.

Remove from the heat and add the salt and pepper. If the mixture is too thick, thin it with a little milk or cream.

Serve the soft polenta hot, with the sliced meat on top.

Danielle's Chocolate Raspberry Tartlets

SIX 4-INCH TARTS

These small tarts were created by Danielle Doyon to be paired with Trois Pistoles Strong Dark Ale, which has a deep, robust flavor. Because the malts for this beer are roasted so vigorously, it ends up with coffee and chocolate notes, making it a perfect match for dark chocolate. The Trois Pistole also has subtle raisin and plum notes, so it worked beautifully with the raspberries in Danielle's tarts.

For the tart shells:

2 cups unbleached all-purpose flour
1 cup confectioner's sugar (powdered sugar)
1/2 teaspoon salt
12 tablespoons cold, cubed unsalted butter (1 1/2 sticks)
1 egg, slightly beaten
1 egg yolk
if necessary: ice-cold water, to be added in tablespoons

Place the flour, sugar, and salt in a food processor and pulse to combine.

Add the butter and pulse until the mixture is sandy.

Add the slightly beaten egg, the additional yolk, and pulse until just moistened. If the dough still seems dry, add one tablespoon of ice-cold water and pulse again until just moistened, adding additional ice-cold water if needed.

Firmly wrap dough in plastic wrap and refrigerate for at least one hour.

Once chilled, divide dough into 6 portions.

Roll out each portion and place each into one of six 4-inch tart pans. Be sure to push dough snugly into the pans. Level off the tops with a dough scraper or a knife for a nice, clean edge. Prick the bottoms of the shells with a fork several times.

Freeze the shells for at least 30 minutes.

Heat the oven to 400°F.

After the shells have frozen, prepare them for baking by weighing them down with actual beans or with metal beans made for weighing down piecrust (cover the tart dough with a piece of aluminum foil, then add the beans).

Bake the tart shells for 15 minutes.

Remove foil and beans and continue to bake the shells for approximately 8-10 minutes more, or until they are golden brown. Allow to cool before filling.

For the tart filling:

11 ounces good bittersweet chocolate
12 ounces heavy cream
2 tablespoons light corn syrup
dash salt
1/3 cup seedless raspberry jam
1 tablespoon butter
2 tablespoons Chambord or other raspberry liqueur, or use raspberry juice

Chop the chocolate and place in a heatproof bowl.

Put the cream, the corn syrup, and the salt in a heavy saucepan over high heat and bring to a boil.

Pour the cream mixture over the chocolate and wait a few minutes to allow it to melt.

Then stir with a whisk, beginning in the center of the bowl.

Next, add the raspberry jam, the butter, and the Chambord or raspberry juice, and stir to combine.

Place a few fresh raspberries in each tart shell, then pour the chocolate filling into the shells.

Refrigerate to set.

If there is any filling left, it can be used to garnish the tarts. Warm filling until it is liquid enough to pour. Place it in a small parchment paper cone and pipe circles all over the top of the tarts.

Danielle also garnishes these tarts with a small heart-shaped sugar cookie, a fresh raspberry, and a sprig of mint.

When it comes to making biscuits, Bob Newell has the touch.

3. Fifty-Two Years in One Kitchen

AFTER EIGHTEEN YEARS, Mike and Neil's A1 Diner has become a destination for food-lovers and diner-lovers, and remains a much-loved part of the local community. Its success, and the acceptance of A1 To Go, have cemented the couple's status in Gardiner as successful businesspeople.

But success hasn't changed Mike and Neil's values. They still work very hard—just not quite all the time. They know that won't change. "This business is a crisis a day," says Mike. He understands the restaurant business. And as much as Mike and Neil have been drivers of growth and change in Gardiner, one of the things that endears them most to the community is their continued appreciation for the past, and their true respect for the people whose hard work was the foundation of today's flourishing diner.

Everyone at the diner, and everyone in town, it seems, is especially happy that the A1 team is still anchored by Bob Newell.

When Bob turned seventy-seven on July 7, 2005, Mike and Neil took him out to dinner. They wanted to honor Bob on his birthday, but with this book in process it seemed natural, too, to honor him for his many years of service. They went to a nice restaurant in Brunswick called Henry and Marty's, whose chef-owners are friends with Mike and Neil. The owners stopped by the table and were delighted to learn Bob's story. Soon everyone in the kitchen had heard about Bob, and when they learned that he had spent fifty-two years in one kitchen, they were mightily impressed. A steady stream of admirers dropped by the table, and they treated Bob like a visiting dignitary.

Which he was.

The kitchen gets busy, but the cooks almost always have fun.

4. Mix All Ingredients

MIKE IS A VERY CREATIVE CHEF with very little disposable time. The result is a whole lot of great recipes that never get written down. "It drives the kids crazy," he says, speaking of his diner staff. "They're always asking about a recipe that's only in my head. I should write more things down, it's true."

As a self-taught chef he has great sympathy for the home cook. "I remember the first time I saw a recipe that said 'cream butter and sugar,'" he says, "I melted it." That does have a certain logic to it, cream being a liquid. Mike was ten years old at the time, so one wouldn't expect him to have had much culinary knowledge. Most of us don't start cooking that early, but every cook needs to begin with the basics.

In the diner's kitchen, Mike has shown dozens of young people with no culinary experience how to become proficient cooks. He shows them a few basic skills—how to use a knife, how to read a recipe. Mike is a master at breaking down a recipe and simplifying it. It's a kind of sport for him to see how short he can make a recipe. The record is a single instruction: "Mix all ingredients."

It gets hot in the kitchen, and the cooks move fast.

5. Muffins Every Morning

I N THE MORNING, PEOPLE WANT MUFFINS. At the diner, the muffins are made from scratch.

"Muffins are one of those things I do by rote every morning," says Mike. "It's the simplest thing in the world." The only part he has to think about is what kind of muffin to make. Often that decision is based on what's available in the kitchen — usually some kind of fruit.

"Once in a while I'll get a new idea," says Mike. When he had some shredded carrots, he used them along with some raisins and walnuts to create a carrot-cake-style muffin. Sometimes he'll do a savory muffin, such as cheddar and bacon. "People are always a little worried about those," Mike laughs.

Mike has been making muffins every day for the past eighteen years. That's a lot of muffins.

"Neil says that everyone who comes in here says these are the best muffins they have ever had," says Mike. "You know why? Because every other muffin in America comes out of the same 30-gallon pail."

He's referring to the pre-made mixes used by so many restaurants today. That practice leads to a homogenization of food that Mike finds both annoying and puzzling. "I never cease to be amazed at the inferior food people will line up to eat," he says. "It tastes the same in Augusta, Maine, as it does in Augusta, Georgia. I guess some people want that."

Mike's frown lifts when he thinks of his growing customer base. "There's a whole part of the population that doesn't want to buy into that," he says. "They want to buy local, and to be more conscious about what they eat. They want a place that makes them feel special, and they want the right value for the right food. They want a unique experience."

On weekdays, breakfast is served until 11:00 A.M. On Sundays, A1 Diner is open only until 1:00 P.M. and serves both breakfast and brunch. Each brunch menu is unique. The menu includes fresh takes on traditional favorites, such as omelets and waffles, along with Mike's more creative dishes. Like Tuscan Poached Eggs, which features prosciutto and Parmesan. Or Moroccan Eggs, in which the poached eggs are served in a warm nest of spinach with yogurt and a drizzle of paprika oil. Even the simple specials are interesting and elegant, like Mike's potato cakes with fresh rosemary and roasted garlic.

Or there are always muffins.

Muffins

ABOUT 10 LARGE MUFFINS or 12 regular-sized muffins
This basic muffin batter can be enhanced with just about any fruit. See below for five variations made at the diner. If you want to be daring, you can try the savory muffins Mike sometimes makes, such as bacon and cheddar.

3 1/2 cups flour
1 cup sugar
1 teaspoon salt
5 teaspoons baking powder
2 eggs
1 1/2 cups milk
2/3 cup vegetable oil

Heat the oven to 350° F.
In a medium bowl, mix the flour, sugar, salt, and baking powder.
In a large bowl, beat the eggs, then add the milk and vegetable oil and stir to combine. Add the flour mixture to the egg mixture and stir to combine.
Stir in any additional ingredients you are using, then put the batter in a greased muffin tin, filling each cup about two-thirds full.
Bake for about 25 minutes, until the muffins have risen and are firm.

Apple Cranberry Muffins: Add 1 apple, peeled and chopped, and 1/2 cup chopped fresh or dried cranberries.

Orange Poppy Seed Muffins: Add the grated peel of one orange, 1 teaspoon orange extract, and 2 tablespoons poppy seeds.

Pear Almond Muffins: Add one pear, peeled and chopped, 1/2 cup toasted slivered almonds, and 1 teaspoon almond extract.

Pear Vanilla Muffins: Add one peeled and chopped pear, and 1 teaspoon vanilla.

Bacon and Cheddar Muffins: Add 8 slices cooked, crumbled bacon and 3/4 cup shredded cheddar cheese.

Garlic Rosemary Potato Cakes

6 LARGE 4-INCH CAKES or about 10 smaller cakes
These are nice for brunch or as a side dish. If your potatoes are very moist, you may find that the potato cakes stick to the pan. In this case, dip the cakes in seasoned flour (flour with salt and pepper added) before frying.

At the diner, Mike places the whole roasted garlic cloves in the mixer, along with everything else, resulting in small chunks of roasted garlic in the finished dish. If you prefer to have the garlic fully incorporated into the mixture, mash the roasted garlic with a fork, then mix with the rest of the ingredients.

8 cloves garlic, peeled
1/4 cup olive oil
2 cups cold mashed potatoes
1 tablespoon fresh rosemary, chopped
2 tablespoons butter

Heat the oven to 350° F.

Place the garlic and the oil in a small ovenproof pan, turn the garlic to coat it with oil, and roast in the oven for about 30 minutes, stirring twice during the cooking period, until the garlic is golden and soft.

Combine in a mixer, or in a bowl using a wooden spoon, the garlic, the oil it was roasted in, the rosemary, and the potatoes. (Mash the garlic first if you want it to be smooth; add it whole if you want it to come out chunky.)

Shape the mixture into cakes with your hands. At the diner, Mike makes the cakes about 4 inches in diameter. You may wish to make smaller cakes, depending on how you plan to serve them.

Fry the cakes in the butter for about 7 minutes on each side, until golden brown on both sides.

This recipe assumes the use of leftover mashed potatoes. If you don't have leftover mashed potatoes and you want to make this dish, mash the potatoes as you would ordinarily, using milk and butter (or other liquid), then chill them.

Tuscan Poached Eggs

2 SERVINGS

This popular brunch dish is best when made with a firm, chewy bread such as the Tuscan Loaf from Maine's Black Crow Bakery.

1/4 cup olive oil
2 cloves finely chopped garlic
1 teaspoon chopped fresh rosemary
4 slices firm, best-quality bread
4 eggs
drop of vinegar, if desired
4 thin slices prosciutto, at room temperature
8 tablespoons freshly grated Parmigiano-Reggiano (or other Parmesan cheese)

Heat the olive oil in a small saucepan or skillet over medium heat. Add the garlic and rosemary and cook just until fragrant, about 2 minutes.

Remove the garlic-rosemary oil from the heat. Spread the oil on both sides of each piece of bread and grill each side. (Use a heavy pan or griddle on the stove, or a panini grill. Or use the oven's broiler, but in this case watch carefully so it does not burn.) Keep the slices warm in the oven or a toaster oven.

Poach the eggs.

When the eggs are almost ready, put two toast slices on each of two plates. Place a slice of prosciutto on each slice of toast. Place a poached egg on top of each slice of prosciutto (make sure to let all the water drain off of each egg). Top each egg with 2 tablespoons grated cheese.

Serve immediately.

*To poach eggs, bring to a boil, in a shallow pan, enough water to cover the eggs. Add a drop of vinegar, if desired, to help stabilize the egg whites. Break each egg onto a small plate, then slide it into the water (that way, if you break an egg yolk, you can discard it or save it for another use without messing up your poaching water). Reduce the heat to a gentle boil and cook for about five minutes, until poached perfectly.

A perfectly poached egg has whites that are set and a yolk that is cooked but still liquid. The unbroken yolk of an egg in this state will have a light-pink color. Of course, if you like your eggs hard, by all means cook them that way.

When the eggs are poached to your liking, lift them out of the water with a slotted spoon, let all of the water drain off, and then proceed with the recipe.

If you prefer, you may use a two-part pan designed for cooking eggs; the top part has indentations to hold the eggs, and it sits over boiling water in the bottom of the pan. Although this pan is called an egg poacher, it actually steams the eggs. It turns out firm eggs with a perfect shape, but they have a tendency to be rubbery. True poached eggs are cooked in water.

6. Dad Will Be Happy with That

THAT CAME OUT PERFECT, JAY."

"Good, so it was just the pan."

It's a quiet Tuesday in the A1 kitchen. Mike holds up the pan in question, one of the new flexible silicone pans.

"This Italian pistachio cake has a tendency to stick, so we tried it in this pan," he says, "but we weren't getting the right results. It wasn't rising properly. We tried a few different things and finally changed to a regular square baking pan." That worked. "A lot of what we do in the kitchen is like detective work," says Mike. "You have to keep looking into it until you figure out what's going on."

Nathan passes by on the way to his work station. "How many lima beans did it say?" Mike asks him. "Two cups dry? Then use four cups of the fresh ones."

Jay puts a big pot on the stove. "Is that for my lobster?" Mike asks.

"No, it's for my chicken," Jay answers. He thinks Mike is joking about the lobster, but then realizes he isn't. "You're making lobster?" he asks.

"Yeah, I have to make lobster stew for my dad." Mike's dad has had an operation and is at the Veterans' Hospital for a few days for rehabilitation. When Mike visited him, the first thing he asked for was some great food—specifically, lobster stew.

Nathan is stemming some Swiss chard.

Bob has finished making the tuna salad. He puts it away and then comes back with a big bowl of corned beef hash. "We make great hash here," he says proudly, then lists off the ingredients. Garlic, onions, potatoes, beef gravy, parsley, celery, and Worcestershire sauce season the corned beef.

"You planning to use the mixer?" Jay asks Mike, getting a No in reply. "I'll do that cake now, then." He's making the second pistachio cake, part of a catering order for A1 To Go.

Mike's lobsters are ready, so he pulls them out and cracks them open, quickly picking out all the meat. He puts some butter in a pan on the stove. "This is my pan," he says. "Nobody touches this pan but me." He adds the lobster and then goes across the room to do something else. Soon the lobster begins sizzling. At the moment when the lobster would start to stick, Mike arrives back at the stove and shakes the pan. He adds more butter, using his fingers to push it around the pan a little. The butter melts together with the juices that are beginning

Mike puts a lot of love into every dish.

to emerge from the lobster meat, the mixture turning a pale pink. Mike heats up some heavy cream on the stove, then adds the lobster mixture to the cream.

"That's really all there is to it," he says, "you just cook the lobster and sauté it in butter, then add heavy cream. I might add some sherry. Just a touch. Sherry is easy to overdo. And it's overused." He sprinkles a little bit of salt into the mixture and tastes it, then pulls out the sherry and adds a very small splash. "I guess it needs just a touch of pepper," he says, adding a tiny amount. He stirs the mixture again and offers a taste. The stew is delicious. There is no discernible taste of sherry or pepper, just a beautiful lobster essence with a subtle creamy flavor that complements it perfectly.

Mike takes a final taste and gives an approving nod. "Dad will be happy with that."

Dad Will Be Happy with That

7. Don't Worry, We've Been Doing This for Years

MIKE GETS UP EVERY DAY AT 5:30 A.M. and comes right into the diner, spending no time at home. It's the only part of the day when there are no interruptions, his "perfect time of day." He makes coffee, then goes to his office below the kitchen to do his morning paper work. "I love that little routine," he says, "it's the way I wake up. Just hearing the sounds of the equipment, the compressor running, all those little sounds that mean the diner. When the floor squeaks, I know someone's in my kitchen. I hear the produce guy drop fifty pounds of potatoes on the floor." By the time he hears the waitress arrive at 6:30 A.M., the perfect time of day is over.

Around this time Danny Chapman comes in for the first coffee run of the day, using the side door and going behind the counter. If there isn't any coffee, he makes some. When Mike hears him he says, "What's going on out there?" Danny replies, "Don't worry, we've been doing this for years."

At 7:00 A.M., Paul Gray is invariably waiting outside. When he sits at the counter for his coffee and donut, Danny might serve Paul's coffee. In that case, Mike puts his head out and jokes, "Who's the new girl?"

The pace picks up when the breakfast crowd thickens. Orders begin to go into the kitchen quickly. Plates emerge from the tiny kitchen window bearing appealing omelets and home fries, beautiful waffles and fruit. Regulars line the stools reading the KJ, as it's known—the *Kennebec Journal*. Early morning meetings take place in some of the booths. The ambient noise rises.

By this time Mike is fully occupied with organizing the day. He makes a shopping list, a food prep list, and a things-to-do list. "The minute I walk through that door I start gathering information," says Mike. "My life is a life of lists."

Around 10:30 A.M., Bob makes the biscuits.

He begins by scooping flour out of a big square blue metal bin that sits on the floor, almost waist high. It looks as though it has been there for decades, and it has—that bin has held that staple for the past sixty years. Bob scoops the flour into the bowl of a large scale, then puts the measured amount into the big Hobart mixer along with the salt, the baking powder, and the shortening. And then he walks away. Bob knows by heart exactly how long it will take.

Soon there will be fresh, hot biscuits.

When Bob senses it is time, he pours in the milk, and a short time later he stops the mixer. Dipping flour again from the bin, he spreads it in a thick white blanket onto his work surface. He removes the bowl from the mixer and scrapes the sticky dough into the flour. With quick, sweeping motions, he pats the dough gently with his hands and a soft, pliant pillow emerges. He dips the rim of a plastic water glass into the flour and uses it to cut the pillow into rounds. He sets these rounds close together on a baking sheet, brushes the tops with melted butter, and puts them in the oven. Then he stays close at hand. About twenty minutes later, hot golden biscuits are calling with their scent.

The lunch crowd varies. Some people just want to get in and get out. Others are there to catch up. On a busy day, you might not get a booth. On a quiet day you might have your pick. On any day, the printed lunch menu carries classic diner fare with great burgers, crispy fries, and the famous onion rings. The meals on the specials board are available at lunch as well. From franks-and-beans to black bean chili, A1 Diner always has something for everyone.

As the day unfolds, a lingering lunch guest can pick up the aromas of the evening's specials being created. There's a whiff of sweet and spicy soy from the Asian noodle broth; these noodle dishes, served initially as specials, have recently been added to the main menu.

An hour later, there's a strong scent of garlic in the air. Kenneth Harrison, the newest member of the kitchen team at A1 Diner, is making a new side dish—sautéed escarole with garlic and lemon juice.

Before moving to Maine recently, Kenneth worked for Tom Douglas, a well-known chef in Seattle. When he describes the contrast between that fast-paced, competitive environment and his situation at A1 Diner, he sounds like a man who has found his home. "This is exactly what I was looking for," he says. "This sort of intimacy with the customer. Seeing someone enjoy the food you have made."

It's a sentiment that has permeated the walls of this diner in every era. People who feed people grow to love them, it seems.

At 4:00 P.M. the kitchen is filled with another wonderful fragrance. Kenneth's lamb will be coming out of the oven soon. He gave it a rub of cumin, coriander, sage, paprika, salt, and brown sugar—it must be the sugar that creates that fascinating hint of caramel in the aroma. A tray of golden toasted orzo looks beautiful. Toasting the orzo gives it a nutty flavor. The orzo will be used with cherry tomatoes in a side dish to accompany Kenneth's salmon special.

These dishes are Kenneth's first addition to the specials menu. He was excited to share them with Mike and Neil for the first time, and the three worked together to formulate exactly the right version of them for the current diner menu.

Kenneth is delighted to be working collaboratively now. "At other places, my voice didn't matter so much," he says. "It was a lot about ego—always vying for attention. Here it is not a competition. You know it's you going out there," he says, meaning that the food he sends out to his customers is entirely in keeping with his personal standards of quality—the standards he shares with Mike and Neil.

At 5:00 P.M. the diner is often quiet. Lunch is well over, the night rush not yet begun. The second-shift dishwasher arrives around this time to dishes in progress. Tori Walsh held this job during her high school years. She remembers it well.

"You come in and you get your apron and your rubber gloves," says Tori, "and you assess the damage. You start with the silverware and the cups and plates—that goes into the old Hobart dishwasher. So you load up the racks and get those going through, and then you sort of look over there with one eye and see what you've got for pots and pans. The worst is when the pastry chef has been there. Then you have the mixers and the dough all in there—that's death for the pot sink, all that dough. But you hurry and get your pots done, because it starts to pick up again within a half hour. And then you're moving with the pace of things, and cracking jokes with whoever is in the kitchen."

The work of the dishwasher is crucial, and a successful restaurant owner respects that. "I tell my dishwashers their role is just as important as anyone else's," says Mike. It's a point on which Maurice Wakefield vehemently agreed with Mike when the two of them met in 2005. The dishwasher is the unsung hero of the kitchen.

As the dinner service progresses, the diner gets busy. In the summer, there's a line on the sidewalk. The customers are a mix of the old and the new, regulars having meat loaf, families ordering mac and cheese for the kids and maybe something traditional for the grownups, or maybe something daring.

A few of the specials and desserts will invariably sell out, and a waitress might be heard to mutter under her breath, echoing Marguerite from years ago, as she removes the bulky menu board from its glass case and carefully takes out the little white letters spelling out Warm Brownie Cup or whatever there is no more of, placing them back in the green wooden box.

Regulars at dinner often chat between booths and the conversation is convivial. In the small space, most conversations can be heard.

And there are private moments as well. Like the time Bill Prindle stopped at the diner on a truly miserable night. With a home in Boston and a summer house in Castine, Maine, Bill and his wife Nina have been traveling to Maine for years in the summer, and they always take the long way so they can stop at A1 Diner. One memorably miserable Friday night, Bill traveled to Maine alone. His mother was gravely ill, he was tired from a long week in a demanding corporate job, and the drive was slow and arduous because of a cold, driving rain. He got to the diner just before closing time and ordered fries with gravy. The hot, comforting food and the warm, familiar diner soothed his soul and made him feel human again.

By closing time, the diner is quiet. It takes an hour or so to clean up, and the last task is mopping the floor. It's a task that Tori, the former dishwasher, remembers with a certain fondness. "At night when everyone left and I would go out there and wash the floor," says Tori, "I looked out those windows and saw my town in a different way." At school, she didn't fit in. At the diner, she was important, and from that experience she gained the sense of a world full of possibilities.

It has been fifteen years since Tori worked at the diner, half her life ago, yet its image is clear in her mind. Remembering the nightly task of closing the diner, she could be speaking for all who have known and loved the place when she relates how it was: "I felt like the diner belonged to me."

Acknowledgments

I am honored to be the one to tell the story of A1 Diner and its forebears. My deepest thanks to Michael Giberson and Neil Anderson for trusting me with this project, and for providing so much guidance and support along the way.

Without the beautiful photography of Jeff Giberson, this book might never have happened. Thanks to Jeff for stepping up to the plate and hitting it out of the park.

Maurice Wakefield was instrumental in helping me understand the early days of the diner, and his daughter, Barbara Emery, provided much support. I am thankful for their generosity.

For sharing their stories of the Gibey era, my deep thanks to Albert and Elizabeth Giberson.

Marguerite Gagne was a crucial source for the Heald's Diner era. I thank her for her candid contributions, and am glad to call her a new friend.

I am deeply grateful to Danny Chapman for his honesty and his insights.

Special thanks to the former diner employees who made such strong contributions to this book: Cindy DeLong, Brian O'Mahoney, Chris Breton, Marlena Klassen, and Tori Walsh.

Thanks to Buffy Parker and Spiros Polemis for a great recipe and a great story.

Many current and former residents of Gardiner supplied tips and tidbits that helped make this book better. Not every story was included, but all of them were helpful. Thanks to everyone who shared their personal stories: Irene Wise, Walter Gosline, Barbara Brown, Kathy Gorham, Clarence McKay, and everyone I have forgotten to mention.

I owe a great debt to the many friends who sustained me throughout this effort, especially Jean McWilliams.

It was my good fortune to team with Tilbury House. Many thanks to my publisher, Jennifer Bunting, for her guidance, her humor, and her vision; to graphic designer Edith Allard for her loving attention to the manuscript and her enthusiasm for the topic; and to my editorial team: Gay Grant for her deft touch, excellent insights, and unfailing support, and Julie Eubanks, for her keen eye, hard work, and great story instincts.

Saving the best for last, the current diner staff made me feel welcome even when I hogged the last booth or got in the way in the kitchen. My thanks to all of you, especially Lisa Lane, Roger Erickson, Matt Rowe, Jay Howard, Kenneth Harrison, and everybody's favorite diner employee for fifty-two years and counting, the sweet and delightful Bob Newell.